BRAVING THE BODY

Edited by Nicole Callihan,
Pichchenda Bao,
& Jennifer Franklin

Harbor Anthologies
Small Harbor Publishing

Braving the Body
Copyright © 2024 by Nicole Callihan, Pichchenda Bao, & Jennifer Franklin
All rights reserved.

Cover art by Megan Merchant
Cover design by Allison Blevins
Book layout by Claire Eder
Project Coordinated by Dustin Brookshire

BRAVING THE BODY
NICOLE CALLIHAN, PICHCHENDA BAO, & JENNIFER FRANKLIN
ISBN 978-1-957248-21-9
Harbor Anthologies,
an imprint of Small Harbor Publishing

Contents

SEAN THOMAS DOUGHERTY
  Why Bother? — 15

Introduction — **17**

JESSICA ABUGHATTAS
  Strip — 21

KIM ADDONIZIO
  Paris — 23

KELLI RUSSELL AGODON
  My Arrhythmia Makes Me Believe I'm Always in Love — 24

LISA ANDREWS
  On the Night the Key Breaks in the Lock — 26

SUBHAGA CRYSTAL BACON
  Fat Shame — 27

CHRISTOPHER BAKKEN
  Negative Theology — 28

MARY JO BANG
  Our Lady of Fire — 29

ELLEN BASS
  Ode to Fat — 30

JEFFREY BEAN
  Under my shirt, above my belt, there's an ache, — 31

JAN BEATTY
    Abortion with Gun Barrel   33

ALLISON BLEVINS
    After Rembrandt's "Self-Portrait," Damaged by Acid in 1977   35

MARINA BLITSHTEYN
    thoth   37

DUSTIN BROOKSHIRE
    When I Was Straight   39

ELENA KARINA BYRNE
    Free Will   41

LAUREN CAMP
    Woman's Body with Birds   42

BRENDA CÁRDENAS
    After Life   44

ROBERT CARR
    Font   46

EILEEN CLEARY
    Flight of the White Throated Sparrow   47

SUZANNE CLEARY
    Emergency Room   48

NADIA COLBURN
    Outside the Sparrows are Awake   49

MARTHA COLLINS
    Like Her Body the World   50

NICOLE COOLEY
    My Mother's Nightgowns Smell Like Smoke   52

JESSICA CUELLO
    Beauty   54

JA'NET DANIELO
    For the Body as Poem   56

JULIA KOLCHINSKY DASBACH
    Why write another poem about the moon?   57

PATRICK DONNELLY
    Prayer Over Dust   59

CAROL DORF
    I used to hold silence. Now I have a lot to say.   61

LIZA KATZ DUNCAN
    Driving South, 10 Weeks Pregnant   63

IRIS JAMAHL DUNKLE
    Dear Body,   64

KATHY FAGAN
    To My Hands On Their Birthday   65

ANN FISHER-WIRTH
    'Tis a Consummation   66

EMILY FRANKLIN
    Plans   67

KAREN FRIEDLAND
    It Recurred   69

SUZANNE FRISCHKORN
    My Body as a Communist Country   70

CMARIE FUHRMAN
    Dear Body   71

JEANNINE HALL GAILEY
    Self-Portrait as a Body Shaped by Illness   73

SONIA GREENFIELD
    All the Women I Know Are Writing Post-Roe Poems   74

DAVID GROFF
  Days of 1986   76

BENJAMIN S. GROSSBERG
  My Mother Approves   78

JARED HARÉL
  Achilles   80

DENNIS HINRICHSEN
  [*lyricism*] [WITH MAY SWENSON AND CECIL THE SPEED DEMON TURTLE]   82

CAMILLE HERNANDEZ
  Hence this Worn Lament   84

KAREN HILDEBRAND
  Secretly, I Named a Flower for You   85

EMILY HOCKADAY
  The Heart Grows Full of Weeds   86

ANDREA HOLLANDER
  Wound   87

JP HOWARD
  in this house   89

JESSICA JACOBS
  Sex, Suddenly, Everywhere   90

MARA JEBSEN
  Deep Water Women   92

MELISSA FITE JOHNSON
  Hereditary   94

PATRICIA SPEARS JONES
  Dancer   95

JEN KARETNICK
On our 31st wedding anniversary, I discover my heart
has hardened,   96

MEG KEARNEY
Duckling, Swan   97

HYEJUNG KOOK
Quick   98

MICHAEL LALLY
I Meant To   100

LANCE LARSEN
Quail Egg   103

VIOLA LEE
Mixtape   105

EUGENIA LEIGH
Gold   106

REBECCA LINDENBERG
The Splendid Body   108

MATTHEW LIPPMAN
The Treasure of the Silence after the Hard Scrabble
Lurch and Lunge for Love   110

MARGAREE LITTLE
Bridle   112

MIA AYUMI MALHOTRA
On Memory   113

CHRISTINE MALVASI
S.A.F.E.   115

CYNTHIA MANICK
Dear Future Body (Keep Your Skin Thickk)   117

FRED MARCHANT
    the burning road   119

JENNIFER MARTELLI
    By August   120

GAIL MARTIN
    Coming Back Body   122

TRAPETA B. MAYSON
    Sweet Mornings   123

CAITLIN GRACE MCDONNELL
    Portrait at 52   125

LYNN MCGEE
    This Is It   127

ERIKA MEITNER
    Touch Cave   129

JENNIFER MILITELLO
    Odaxelagnia   131

SAMANTHA MOE
    I can't see you by the shore anymore but I pretend you're
    still here/ we make dinner for our children   132

FIA MONTERO
    Diastasis Recti Abdominis   134

CARIDAD MORO-GRONLIER
    To the Childhood Friend who Shrugged when *Roe vs Wade*
    was Overturned because She Claimed to Have No Skin
    Left in the Game   135

MARY MORRIS
    Appointment with Dr. Siegel   137

ALICIA REBECCA MYERS
    Giving Birth May Alter a Mother's Bones   138

RACHEL NEVE-MIDBAR
  Somewhere Within   139

JOSHUA NGUYEN
  After I Was Mistaken for the Stripper While Delivering
  Barbeque to an All-White Bachelorette Party   141

REBECCA HART OLANDER
  Anniversary   143

LISA OLSTEIN
  The Spell   145

ALIXEN PHAM
  It Happens All the Time on the Serengeti   146

MAYA PINDYCK
  Addendum   148

IAIN HALEY POLLOCK
  All the Possible Bodies   149

CONNIE POST
  Citadel   150

VIVIAN FAITH PRESCOTT
  Tracking the Animal   152

ROBIN REAGLER
  Contradictions in a Landscape of Human Love   154

SUSAN RICH
  Post-Surgical Love Sonnet   155

MICHAEL ROBINS
  The Ordinary Inexplicable   156

ANNA V. Q. ROSS
  All my poems used to end in sky   157

CHRISTOPHER SALERNO
  Headfirst   159

HAYDEN SAUNIER
    Performing Heart Surgery at 2 A.M. While Asleep   161

DIANE SEUSS
    My hair? Oh, the color of a field mouse.   163

JACKIE SHERBOW
    Razor Burn   165

BETSY SHOLL
    Thinking of Richard Avedon's Portrait of Isak Dinesen   166

DARA-LYN SHRAGER
    Wednesday Bronchitis   168

NOEL SIKORSKI
    In the car on the way to a family reunion   169

DREW SKELTON
    Odonostalgia   171

MONICA SOK
    The Hallway   173

JOANNA SOLFRIAN
    Mount Sinai   174

DONNA SPRUIJT-METZ
    Dead Fathers Club   175

HEATHER SWAN
    Resurrection of the Body   176

KELLY GRACE THOMAS
    A Fertility Clinic is the Coldest Place on Earth   177

LYNNE THOMPSON
    My Body Leaning Into   178

KC TROMMER
    Agency   180

MICHAEL TYRELL
   Intruder   182

LEAH UMANSKY
   Reckoning   183

BARBARA UNGAR
   AP Physics   184

LEE UPTON
   Why Am I Not Invited to Your Party?   186

SARA WALLACE
   Thirty Years   187

JESSICA L. WALSH
   It's Normal to Feel Your Body Has Betrayed You   189

PATRICIA J. WENTZEL
   Miracle Weight Loss Drugs   190

ZOË RYDER WHITE
   Eleven Impossibilities   192

REN WILDING
   Snakeskin   193

MARIANNE WORTHINGTON
   Low Ground of Sorrow   194

JUSTIN WYMER
   After, Still, I Want Someone to Want My Body   196

Acknowledgments   **199**

Contributor Bios   **207**

Editor Bios   **237**

About Small Harbor Publishing   **239**

Braving the Body

Why Bother?

Because right now, there is someone

out there with

a wound in the exact shape

of your words.

—*Sean Thomas Dougherty*

Introduction

Dear Reader,

    I love letters. I love the ones on hotel stationery and the ones on the free greeting cards from rural Maine libraries; the ones scrawled on college-ruled paper and sketched on the backs of postcards from Galveston. I love the canceled stamps, the stuffed shoe boxes, the sprigs of lavender. I even love the ones never sent and the ones still awaiting a reply. There is something in knowing that a hand—*your hand*—picked up a pen—a favorite pen, a borrowed pen, any pen—and wrote these words in a particular order on a particular morning in a particular body.

    And perhaps even more, I love poems: their *tender Majesty*, as Emily Dickinson would say, those letters to the world which contain the images—the sights and sounds and felt moments—that serve as evidence of embodied existence: a lemon grated for its zest; or—as found in this collection—Mary Morris's "blouse flowering with milk" and Justin Wymer's, "pill the color of her hair." It is only through the body that we receive images, and mostly through the images that we receive poems.

    Braving the Body is a collection of such poems; of 116 bodies; of, as Whitman writes in *Leaves of Grass*, "head, neck, hair, ears . . . mouth, tongue, lips . . . bowels sweet and clean . . . brain in its folds inside the skull frame . . . heart valves;" of Liza Katz Duncan's 10-week pregnant body driving south; of the cast made of Drew Skelton's teeth; the discarded membranes of Fia Montero's "Diastasis Recti Abdominis;" the imagined daffodils planted by "our children's children" of Ann Fisher-Wirth's final consummation with her beloved.

This book was born out of the work from my book *This Strange Garment*, published by Terrapin Books in early 2023, a book which reckoned with my experience of a stage 2 bilateral breast cancer diagnosis in September 2020 (yes, *that* 2020; deep in a pre-vaccine pandemic). In the months after, during treatments and surgeries, I wrote poem after poem, even thumbing one into my phone in the Intensive Care Unit. And all the while, the poems felt bigger than me; they didn't have that slight solipsistic feel poems sometimes have; they felt *of the body*, of the larger concerns of what it means to get to go on living, and witnessing, and smelling, and tasting.

One January afternoon, having just left radiation treatment, I stood on the corner of Broadway and 14th Street; the snow stung my face the tiniest bit; I ate a street taco and mustered the strength to walk to Chinatown to buy burn cream. And, that day, walking to Chinatown—dropping a letter in a blue box along the way—I felt so alive. Even now, nearly three years later, I can almost hear the rhythm in my slow steady steps: *I'm alive, I'm alive,* and looking around at the passersby: *you are alive, and you; we are alive, we are here; we have made it this far and that matters.*

When *This Strange Garment* was published, I knew I wanted to honor the experience in a way that extended beyond my own experience in my own body. I reached out to Thomas Dooley of New York City's *Poetry Well*, an organization committed to celebrating and promoting poetry as a vital part of individual and collective wellness. I thought we might set up a reading! But the idea grew and grew. I reached out to Jennifer Franklin and Pichchenda Bao—two poets I deeply admire for their own writing about their own bodies—and asked if they wanted to join us in our thinking: *a series of conversations perhaps? maybe a call for online poems?* Way led on to way; we hosted a summer conversation series and an ekphrastic experience at the Metropolitan Museum of Art; we found space for readings and community sharing; we put out a call for poems; submissions poured in—over 2,500 poems—, each of which Jenny and Chenda and I read, so many of which we admired, and thus, the difficult, electric selection process, to create *Braving the Body*. Ultimately, we found a home with Harbor Editions, a publisher who radically accepts each and all of the bodies contained herein; all the gore and glory; the dizzying spectrum of health and illness; the fluid stretch of gendered embodiment; the lines that spill and spill (& spill) outside the margins. I am profoundly grateful to Allison Blevins and Dustin Brookshire for making the space for this collection—absurd, sublime, anxious, and tender—in which the poems resonate in the very place they were born—the brave, brave body—and which, you, Dear Reader, now hold in your hands.

I'm thinking of Baby Suggs in Tony Morrison's *Beloved*: "In this here place, we flesh, flesh that weeps, laughs; flesh that dances on bare feet in grass. Love it. Love it hard . . . You got to love it. This is flesh I'm talking about here. Flesh that needs to be loved." And, let it be so. Let the body and its images, its longings and hungers, its sternum and its constellations of freckles be loved. Dear Body. Dear, dear Body. Dear Reader, I'm thinking of you—

    N.

JESSICA ABUGHATTAS

Strip

To remove all contents or possessions from
To empty completely
A sequence of images telling a story
A main road in or leading out of a town
A long narrow shape (especially of a woman)
To tear the thread or teeth from
To dispossess, leave bare, remove all coverings
To press the eggs from (a splayed fish)
To gut
To remove bark and branches from (an olive tree)
To remove the midrib from (its leaves)
To milk (a cow) to the last drop
To barefoot the child always drawn from behind
To deprive someone of
To take away from, confiscate
To rob, ravage, ransack, raid, reave, rifle
To fire a bullet from a rifled gun
To rip the sheets from a bed
To lay bare, devastate, sack
To tease
Example: prisoners, down to their underwear
To denude; delude
To divest
To remove the fittings of or take apart (a machine) to inspect it, to
    adjust it
Example: a tank piece by piece
To dismantle, disassemble, demolish, deny

To take to pieces, take to bits, take apart, break up
To recall Al-Dawayima, Deir Yassin, Hula, Tarshiha, Jish
To clear, clean out, loot, pillage, plunder
To, often polemically, insist on nuance
To paint Gernika upon a camp entrance
To make the body believe lies about itself
To hear over a megaphone in one's native tongue today is judgment day
To sell off for profit
To use for or involve in performance
To hundred dollar bill
To entertain
To scatter like the people of Sheba
To desire no sense of permanence
To undress
Suddenly and into the dead dead sea

KIM ADDONIZIO

Paris

After her fall Terrel got a glass eye that when she wore it looked so
    perfect
you'd never guess it wasn't real but by the time it was made she preferred
to wear one of her patches, at first pirate black but then silver or glittery
gold, they suited her so well we all admired her and when the cancer
news hit her—I was about to say *blindsided* her, suddenly not a
    metaphor—
she fucked off to Paris with Porter for a vacation and that was so her,
we all agreed, that group of us who got together over dinner
every few weeks and there was always someone who someone knew or
heard of who'd died, or was nearly there, maybe just so old or in the
    hospital, our
custom during each story was to knock our wineglasses together and
    proclaim *We're*
alive! In the end—if that's an end—the cancer scare was just that, not
    so dire,
after all. Would you prefer the darkness—who knows what horror
will greet us next, like a concierge with a condescending stare—
or the lemon soufflé? Wherever we're going, we're already nearly there.

KELLI RUSSELL AGODON

My Arrhythmia Makes Me Believe I'm Always in Love

Like Jiffy Pop on the hot
   stove, all those kernels

glowing POP hot, everyday
    like that   holding

the door open for a jean jacket
   woman in black boots

telling the cashier   no
   bag   my heart a tote

of bees my heart   fluttering
   at the sunrise sunset   your

hand around or not
   around my waist   all

those years I heard
   my neighbor playing his drums

the vibration   through the walls
   of my lungs   my desire

irregular   each ventricle
a hummingbird feeder filled

with wings.

LISA ANDREWS

On the Night the Key Breaks in the Lock

Everything, the locksmith said, *has its breaking point.*
A telephone, a camera, a marriage — I don't understand
how anything works. Heart or eye. Mind, mouth, or throat.
The numerous small bones. How difficult swallowing can be;
how it isn't that hard to choke. By which I mean, of course,
the opposite. The body's potential for betrayal so vast,
we ought to applaud it every day, praise all things that work,
and do no harm. Music without static. Elections not hacked.
The homeless man who leapt in front of you — signal and gate
between you and the car you never saw coming. But who
sees anything coming? I mean the thing that comes
from nowhere — the shuddering sky, the distance
between you and the shore: riptide — where water divides
against itself and you. Your husband carrying you
along the rift in the ocean's side. Your husband also
who intervened on the FDR — while you bent down and braced
for the impact you thought inevitable — the optimist who married you
reached for the cab driver, calmly and firmly showing him
where to look, and what to do. Thank them both.
Celebrate and acknowledge all the nights in your life
you have slept. Praise everything benign, indolent —
chronic, even. The water you can drink at your lips.

SUBHAGA CRYSTAL BACON

Fat Shame

Over breakfast, I read about *Fat Eater,* the latest Shark
Tank discovery, a *totally natural and organic pill* that eats
fat. The video shows a woman in beige underwear
lifting her belly onto a tabletop. I know it's wrong.
Later in town, from the bakery came a woman
in stretchy clothes, round everywhere, carrying a cake.
Fat Eater I thought.
                    My father's mother had a big soft body
with thin arms and legs. She was always *heavy*
is the word we used. So my mother warned *you'll end up
as big a mom-mom.* When I asked for seconds at table,
she would say my name and puff out her cheeks.

I got the message. All my life, I've watched my weight—
watched it increase my mother would say. My partner
from some years ago had a high round belly and received
an anonymous letter describing a diet. *It really works*
someone had written. It was her birthday. I had bought
a special cake—the letter hung in the air with candle smoke.

On TV, there's a woman whose character has *struggled
with weight* since childhood: emotional eating, body image
and so on. How see her life as a fight when, as I watch her
in my loose sweats, she moves like a body of water,
her beauty not diminished by her girth. Watching her
I try to shed the shame fed to me since birth.

Negative Theology

Case in point: the ear's empty theater.
Or the relentless, metered heart.

The unseaworthy trireme of the brow.
Even the pelvis and its one want.

Always mounting, the evidence against us.
Case in point: the insufficient foot.

We don't know anything. Yet here, again,
the sun's perpetual choir, silent as ever.

Proof enough to keep us guessing.
Plenty to fill our sad little urns.

Reaching with all the strength I never had
both shadows and fire drain through my fingers.

MARY JO BANG

Our Lady of Fire

I sometimes feel I'm encompassed in fire—
the heat that hollows the building
once the arsonist says, "Bye-bye girls,
just do what you want," to the gas can
and match. I don't believe in fate and yet,
how can you argue against who you are?
The fire is almost out, the match gone,
and the gas can flattened by falling timbers
when the arsonist circles back
to see what the damage has done. Once,
next to a river, I saw something in the grass,
a pin in the shape of an animal. I picked it
up, I put it on. I wore it until one day I saw
it was worthless: that it had only ever been
a moment between sleeping in one bed
and waking in another. And yet, the butterfly
it was, inexpensive alloy, mother-of-pearl
inlay, had been a form of evidence—that I,
a body, had been there, that night, time
above me, air around me, light reflecting
off the river a line of silver that held no hint
of the horrors racing toward me: my name
in ink on a heat-seeking missile sent
from an unseeing heaven, the gods asleep.

ELLEN BASS

Ode to Fat

Tonight, as you undress, I watch your wondrous
flesh that's swelled again, the way a river swells
when the ice relents. Sweet relief
just to regard the sheaves of your hips,
your boundless breasts and marshy belly.
I adore the acreage
of your thighs and praise the promising
planets of your ass.
Oh, you were lean that terrifying year
you were unraveling, as though you were returning
to the slender scrap of a girl I fell in love with.
But your skin was vacant, a ripped sack,
sugar spilling out and your bones insistent.
Oh, praise the loyalty of the body
that labors to rebuild its palatial realm.
Bless butter. Bless brie.
Sanctify schmaltz. And cream and cashews.
Stoke the furnace
of the stomach and load the vessels. Darling,
drench yourself in opulent oil,
the lamp of your body glowing. May you always
flourish enormous and sumptuous,
be marbled with fat, a great vault that
I can enter, the cathedral where I pray.

JEFFREY BEAN

Under my shirt, above my belt, there's an ache,

a pain in my gut no doctor can explain.
It stays. And is blue. Blue as sprays

of sidewalk salt beneath the steel bells
of the Catholic Church, blue as noon-light

enflaming stained glass. Slate-blue
of gravestones, morning sky

before snow. In my gut there is the blue
of the blue whale's heart, size of a golf cart,

the lips of a child swimming in Lake Michigan
at night. Blue of a dead man's fingers, navy

crayon melted on a dashboard, dusk
at the end of a wasted day, smart phone blazing

with blue-lit news that can't be ignored: more
violence, more disgrace. In my gut, a seagull

pecks at a Pepsi can in a Kroger parking lot,
a jail cell's metal door slams closed

in fluorescent light, sanitary paper crinkles
on a medical exam table. In my gut, a summer

basket of blueberries, a field of cornflowers
writhing in wind. Bolt of cloth in the corner

of the flag where the stars go, Viagra rattling
in a plastic bottle, passed through the pharmacy

drive-through window. In my gut, grandfathers
splash on Aqua Velva and lean in blue blazers

at parties, drinking tumblers of vodka on the rocks.
Cerulean locker room cinderblocks, police-light blue,

three-day-old bruise blue, denim on college boys
roaring at a basketball game. In my gut is the blue

of the brightest star in Canis Major, Sirius,
the dog star, a binary, a double-blue dog that haunts

sheds by the railyard, hovers over my driveway
when I can't sleep. Blue of the filled-in bubbles

on standardized tests, blue of smeared handprints
on bus windows. Fish blue, breathless

blue, icicle blue. Blue of the sapphire
in the ring of the slaughtered king,

dropped to the bottom
of the Aegean.

JAN BEATTY

Abortion with Gun Barrel

The 12 year-old walks thin, like a child/
her hair alive in vibrating threads
in the clinic light.
Her mother: *My daughter. I give my permission.*
And the girl cannot be real, or the sky
would burn—not bleed like it does in
the waiting room of grown women.
The mother in the brittle inner office scribbles
her name small on the collapsing form.
Now move the flying hands of the counselor
who becomes the first bird,
stripping the sky blank with air leaving.
Now she walks back to the maze of illuminated
bodies to find a way to make herself dissolve:
Not what I wanted for you, not this.
In the inner body of the clinic, the divining
of this choice: the small name solid,
the songbird stopped/
the singing continues.
I am the counselor,
there are cracks in the barrel of the gun/
there is aiming/
shots of sorrow—
shots of light.
I am ruinous with light, we are ruinous with making
our lives in the procedure room.
The 12 year-old opens the leaving door—

a bird let loose, no clear note to sing.
Song of sorrow and praise as she wears
the skin of herself,
this idea of skin that she's learning.

After Rembrandt's "Self-Portrait, Damaged by Acid in 1977"

I.

A woman opens and closes window curtains inside the tight walls of her childhood bedroom. A green orb explodes behind her clenched eyelids—chemical stars packed into shells, propelled by gunpowder and flame. I can't remember how I learned to masturbate in this room, girl young and blue with fresh wanting. Handle properly or risk serious injury, even death.

II.

My daughter clenches melting chocolate in her right hand, a wad of yellow chrysanthemum trailing root and dirt in her left. She wears a pink leotard and my black Jackie Os upside-down on her deep-sloped nose. Mothers struggle with the crisp sunshine, with certainty. At forty, will my daughter still walk? Understand the overflowing burden of blur and tremor? I won't live to see her.

III.

A young deer chases a blackbird in the empty lot beside the hospital parking lot. I fucked a boy on a picnic table next to a pond one teen-drunk Saturday night. I don't remember his hands or name. The animal body is liquid. I'm supposed to feel hopeful—as if some moments belong just to me. Remember how the mist from peeled citrus saturates skin for days after you've swallowed its crisp pulp.

IV.

My postpartum depression wasn't your fault and other apologies I never spoke race in my liquid medicine guts. I want to mail you postcards from the bedroom but we keep the stamps in the kitchen. As a girl, I spent my days in dance class. That body still lives inside this body. *You're so much more flexible than I expected*, says the physical therapist. I'm insulted.

V.

Imagine every body as a widow-maker heart, blue and pulsing, waiting for interrogation— how pain speaks to legs or torsos or eyeballs. What is left in my body to confess? Hot iron, rack, pear, rats, boot, prod, chair, ice, shock, whip, thumbscrew, rope. Perhaps the space around a body in pain matters more than the body itself. I tell my son we only understand happiness because of death.

MARINA BLITSHTEYN

thoth

there is a scale
there is a scale to my sins
a feather for every
a scale for the weakness i pick at all day like a drug
a sin on my skin, a prick of the spindle, a bug
i'm pregnant with these
a scale for them all
my height and my hair
my cadences
how much i smile
a scale for the faults in my face
a scale for the lines on my thighs
dig deep, a scale for a slice of my thumb
how far can you go down the well
where the water's worth more than the pail
how far in the breath when it goes
how slow out the breath when it falters
a kingdom for these, a crown
a scale for a scale
how slither, how shed
how keep myself up like a cow
a body a cow, an utter
and offal, and smell
and a tell and a tic, a tail
to hide in my hide, to itch
at my habits, to eat at them
oink to ink, to ash at them

mule to bone, to breastfeed them
tooth and all, to mother them
wild and godless

DUSTIN BROOKSHIRE

When I Was Straight

after Maureen Seaton

I stayed home
while my mother
drove to the grocery store.
Two hours alone to prance
in my mother's high heels,
wear her dresses and nightgowns,
and a white t-shirt as a wig.
I'd probe her jewelry box,
slip on a ring or two,
a necklace, and the bracelet
she only wore for special occasions.
Sometimes I applied
her lipstick with a smile.
I'd sit back straight, legs crossed
directing the household staff
that we didn't have
on the tasks of the day:
vacuum, mop, polish the china,
and press the laundry—
a boss lady before
being a boss lady was a thing.
I'd twirl around the living room
with one hand extended,
an invitation to a man
who wouldn't enter my life
for another thirty-five years.

When I was straight,
my father would say,
*I'd rather one of my sons
blow my brains out
than tell me he is gay.*

Free Will

A neighbor boy took me down to his family's basement bomb shelter, handed me his fear without permission. I'll find pyre sticks and yard death stones furred in dirt. My hands, animals that bleed at the teeth. Building one fort before dusk, the splintered wood will squint back at me before imploding. I am teaching myself how to fight, to spell and run the twelve-year-old enemy home. A young body knows the borrowed physics from the future, the way this desert landscape offers mirages at the end of our street: dusk, trailing its sulphur ghosts back into the underworld of adults. I know now how winter days scattered the broken furniture of trees, passed acres of water through the gutters and expelled its unrolled runic map under my feet. My head molecules would expand, lose all shape. I keep thinking about it. Did you know we wouldn't live if it weren't for the sky's downward pressure per pound, down upon us, the body pushing back?

LAUREN CAMP

Woman's Body with Birds

As she talks, I am not looking exactly
at the small crowd of stitches
scattered like bird prints on her torso,
or the arched dash of migrating tracks
where a doctor drew into her coast with a knife.

Last night, my body learned appeasement.
As the moon slouched, I again stretched
the soft parts of me that curve,
while the unscripted night turned in cycles.

In the locker room as she turns to the side,
I see her naturally sturdy self
settling, repairing.

Last night, he pushed against bone,
held my mind in his palms.

When the doctor told her it must go,
I imagine the breast sat like a bird on the dock
of her naked frame, beating
the precise rhythm of lament —

and if it bothered to flutter little wings
even once for the journey ahead,
it was in thin bright tones of uncertainty.

Because it is rude, I am not looking,
but I know her blood keeps pumping, even there.

For minutes I hold the colors of my breath.
When I walk away, fully dressed,
I reach to touch the two nests of cells on my chest,
to lift them up, and pull in tight.
The arc of my gestures is close to my body.

BRENDA CÁRDENAS

After Life

Perhaps our ghosts wear the sequined sarongs
and turquoise plumes we would never don in life—
string bikinis in the grocery store checkout,
crystals squinting from our belly buttons,
campfire red hair wind-tossed and tangled.

Perhaps we laugh so hard, we snort in public,
sweat splashing on a stranger's perfumed skin.
We swing our Botero hips, pucker crimson lips
for kisses from passersby. We befriend all
the invisible canines nipping at our skinless heals.

Perhaps we dance Limbo, lowering the stick,
no worry for pulled hamstrings or broken backs,
so we shimmy and twist, play air guitar on our ribs,
hit the mosh pit, body slam and body surf.
We call in sick, perhaps we never go to work.

Perhaps we lick the nape of a lost lover's
neck, just to remind them we once tangoed
in the blooming garden of their chest before
neglecting to pull weeds or water thirsty roots.
Perhaps we envelop them with quiet amends.

Perhaps our ghosts sip martinis and toast the stars,
awake all night, lake lapping in our conch shell ears,
endless blue-black waters echoing the loon's

tremolo, its seamless switch in pitch to remind us
that another is always present on a distant shore.

ROBERT CARR

Font

I like your blonde curls in bar light. The silver
foil peels from a beer. There's a little ocean

in your green eyes, a lot of sad. You talk about the drive
down from Skowhegan, pulling over twice so he

could heave. A long day of waiting at Maine Medical,
beloved backbones a constant reminder the body once

had weight. I take you to my room, the Motel 6 in Portland.
You whisper how he's lost the strength to walk, so for weeks

you've carried him like a child learning a waltz. You tell me how,
lifted from the bed, he places lesioned soles on top of your feet,

how you walk backward toward the bathroom, how in all
those weeks you haven't cried. You roll white socks,

slip them into Reeboks. After apologetic sex, I tell you,
Get up. Towering, I tell you, *Put your feet on mine.* Arms

wrapping shoulders, cheek against chest, I walk us
to the motel window, listen to your jag of breath,

whimper of weeping for a man I'll never meet. I memorize
the font of a red 6, the cigarette smell of your hair.

EILEEN CLEARY

Flight of the White Throated Sparrow

As tall as a table when my mother told me
the dead someday return. I cast earth,
fists dirt-full. One to the next, I feed the trees,

flap my hands, but do not fly. Any god may
assume habits of a white-throated sparrow
and need not explain why. I ask maples

if they miss the bodies they drop. Miss
their quietudes. I carry their red deaths,
entomb them in wax paper. After years

apart, the state brings my brothers
and sisters to visit. It's almost as if we're alive.

SUZANNE CLEARY

Emergency Room

When it's your heart you go to the front of the line,
ahead of the hump-backed woman holding a rosary
and the construction worker holding his side
and the woman with long brown hair holding a baby.
You go ahead of the boy with his arm in a towel,
his father holding a cellphone and not looking up.
You walk two steps and then you feel a wheelchair
at the back of your knees, and you sit. I sat.
The florescent light seemed to shimmer like a bead
curtain, and I'm not saying that I saw my life flash
before me, but next I was seeing that day in Rome
when I stood inside the front door of my hotel
watching rain, sudden and hard, fall,
and that old man appeared with a blue plastic bucket
full of umbrellas. How happy I was, I remembered,
to have my choice of colors: red, blue, black, yellow.
I chose a red one, then I put it back, I wanted
the yellow. Everyone on our tour was choosing,
and my husband helping me open the cheap
overpriced umbrella, as rain beaded on my glasses
and it became clear that we would let
nothing stop us, not that day.

NADIA COLBURN

Outside the Sparrows are Awake

and all the complications in my heart:
I, who did not know how to love
my own body, who mistook
the world for a task. Listen:
one voice and then another
amid the rustling of the leaves.

MARTHA COLLINS

Like Her Body the World

hit and hit and hit and hit and fallen

getting up and trying to get up

now one part is hitting another part wounding its flesh

slicing its own veins breaking its bones

but wait we are coming help is on the way

now we are hitting the part that is hitting the part

now it is arm against arm hand against hand

now it is eye against eye no one can see

now it is ear against ear there is no mouth

where is the up to get up to where is the body

where are the parts have the parts all fallen apart

we are part of the body we forgot

we thought we lived outside like a brain in a jar

we thought we were pure like thought with nothing to lose

but we are losing too we are losing parts

besides we were never that brain we were only a part

we thought we would never fall but we are falling

falling and falling and falling hitting the air

falling hitting ourself our own body

meanwhile the body the world will try to get up

or else the body the world   will lie down

NICOLE COOLEY

My Mother's Nightgowns Smell Like Smoke

White cotton, with buttons the size of baby teeth.

Each morning, in one of her nightgowns and my black winter boots, I drive my daughters to school, and as they climb out of the car, I want to crawl out of my own skin, everything prickly and hesitant.

*

I'm on the elliptical trainer at the YMCA beside my younger daughter who wears a black Thrasher t-shirt. She doesn't skateboard, doesn't live in California. And a few days later on my way to fly to my father after my mother dies I see many teen girls in the airports I pass through wearing that exact shirt. *Skateboarding is a dangerous sport. You could break bones,* I caution my daughters that night from New Orleans on the phone as I sit on my parents' bed, in the house without my mother, as if now I could protect anyone's fragile body.

*

We called them the guilt skirts, the three skirts she sewed for me when I broke up with my graduate school boyfriend and she knew she didn't help me when I cried. She mailed me the skirts instead. One with flowers, one green, one gray. I never wore them. Now the skirts hang bunched in my closet beside my daughter's prom dress.

*

In New Orleans, my mother has been dead for three days, and I wake up and my hands are shaking and my sister and I drive to the Salvation Army Family Store on Jefferson Highway and drop off another trash bag of her clothes. *It's my happy place,* I tell my sister and I am being ironic and *using humor as a coping mechanism* as at least one grief podcast recommends but it's also true, and she agrees, as we finger racks of dresses. We can't leave till I find something that is a channel back to her. In the dressing room, I sweat through velvet in someone else's too tight blouse.

*

The fake French café where I have disappeared to write about my mother in Brooklyn is advertising "Bastille Day Specials" and I remember the first Bastille Day in New Orleans in 1976, and how my mother sewed my sister and me can-can dresses: satin and rainbow nylon net to kick up in ruffled layers. All summer, we wore the dresses every day and slept in them, in our twin beds, in our girl bodies, when we were still daughters.

JESSICA CUELLO

Beauty

I suspected beauty in myself, I broke the bathroom

sink trying to reach the mirror, longed for photos,

there were none. I was an observer of my own knees,

stroked my own thighs, my arms the same delicate

slope as the shell split open to reveal the whorl,

the tiny empty rooms shrinking into themselves.

I was beautiful to dogs, they bit me, they wanted

my flesh. One tore open my calf, a dog on a chain

broke free to nip me. *They can smell your fear. So*

stop fearing, the man said as his dog leapt on

his leash. The man choked him back. The beauty

in me could break a home by standing still or scare

a man by spitting milk into his lap. My cry could

rupture love. I wandered through a mother's house

to find a picture of my face, mine could crack

and split your mouth, break the frame, and it is so plain

to see, in the womb I was an egg that should have spread

its blood and thinned, ugliness thrust its way to me, a banal

fist and slap and now my form must be erased, and beauty

keeps attracting gropes, the Salvation Army clerk who thought

I was a thief and lifted up my shirt where the bare ribs

were and the skirt where she sought the necklace.

I had not stolen. I froze for any caress, any

glance. Rough like my origin. Yes, even if

it pinched, accused. My beauty was criminal,

it begged. It said *Break my skin to make it seen.*

JA'NET DANIELO

For the Body as Poem

I was searching for the metaphor—something about
tumor as bird or star, or the space between bones,
breath. Interstitium. Didn't scientists call this
a new organ, this thing that's always been
beneath the skin, holding us together? I wandered
through your rooms, stumbled upon an overturned
chair in the kitchen, an overturned miniature chair
on the dresser—microcosm inside a microcosm.
I lost myself in laundry, in the sketch of a buck
on the wall, in fat yellow flowers on red wallpaper.
I thought about night, about wind, how today,
I called my co-workers *unimaginative.* I tried to imagine
you, to close my eyes & see your imprint behind
my lids, your mottled specks & blotches. When my
vitreous detached, my eye lit up with flash. For months,
a blurred spot floated back & forth across my retina. It
reminded me of you.

JULIA KOLCHINSKY DASBACH

Why write another poem about the moon?

because you wake exhausted of your own
body and its sea as far as mother

from tranquility because the moon too
can't refuse her tether in every sky

as your children scream for you and moon
as though your bodies were both

soft and certain and your daughter's
skin is speckled strawberry

from frozen fruit and some
mysterious rash between her spine

and hairline and you think how beautiful
the rise and fall of her dusted surface

because when the new moon moves
between Earth and sun she leaves

a tail of sodium and our
planet pinches that stream invisible

because we are wrapped in salt
and moon is moo is milk is me is me meaning

every moon poem is your way of making
moon into Mama and back again

stone to shine to disappear without
your children ever knowing you were gone

PATRICK DONNELLY

Prayer Over Dust

Into the kitchen bucket
go the bitter carrot tops,
collard ribs, burned heels,
drain-catcher leavings, useless
skins of things or their stringy hearts.

To these I've begun to add
my nail clippings and clumps
of hair that catch in the brush,
a way my mind chooses
to practice a hard thing.

But my body has lost interest
in the distinction between
Me and Not Me, rushes ahead
to the black box in the yard
with the mail-order worms:
fungus rings germinate
in my dark, moist places,
rash flashes up my torso,
my tongue wears white scum
and a sour, clabbered smell.

You, who cause the chemistry
of things coming apart
to give off an almost social warmth—
when it's over, let my body

be useful, let little bears
nose through my guts
for grubs, let Destroying Angel
lift its wild orchid umbrella
where my heart used to be.

CAROL DORF

I used to hold silence. Now I have a lot to say.

for Stinson Beach

Sun canopies and umbrellas –
breaking waves, lines of surf

I realized I had forgotten how to walk –
the alternation of limbs
the propulsion through space

On the sociable side of the beach
one Dalmatian and a pit bull mix

High above a string of pterodactyls
in formation or maybe just pelicans
flew into the afternoon light

Once I walked to the tide pools
today I narrate into a phone

So many children crying
at the end of the day wanting something
that's been left behind

I say, *this is Carol and it's Sunday*
into your empty machine

A cluster of preteens
throw something back and forth
and shriek — is it dead?

Did I mention light's reflection
on sand as well as water?

Driving South, 10 Weeks Pregnant

Delaware bleeds into Maryland bleeds
into Virginia into West Virginia into Virginia
again. These nauseating hills. This endless

highway, mountained on both sides.
*If something were to go wrong. If I were
to bleed. If I were to need a doctor.*

These pregnant hilltops, straining against
the punishing pink sky. Clouds spooling
and unspooling. How anyone can mistake

this country for beautiful. *If I couldn't
reach a doctor in time. If there
were no doctor. If no doctor would see me.*

How shadows blue the mountains
at sunset. How fireflies dot the grass.

IRIS JAMAHL DUNKLE

Dear Body,

1. this is a blurry love letter.
   [See examples in Mary Shelley's *Frankenstein*.]

2. For so long you have been my far-off star;
   the sword I swallowed [made of fire?] and walked on.

3. And you scarecrowed the pulse of my mind.

4. There were days when electricity could thread
   your pulse awake and you'd bloom
   like a goddamned peony   [See Elizabeth Bishop's "The Fish"].

5. Body, let's be real, I never trusted those raves of force.
   I knew you'd sink back into being a sheath, something to shed –
   My poisonous snake.

6. I'm writing to tell you, those little nerves you wove back into my legs
   like new galaxies are my new true loves.

7. And those webs of muscle they've constructed that carry me
   are my beloveds.

8. I am walking into the new year like it is a starving ocean
   not knowing if you, body, are my master or servant
   [See Kate Chopin's *The Awakening*].

9. Dear Body, Dear Body, Dear Body—I promise this time not to
         forsake you—

KATHY FAGAN

To My Hands On Their Birthday

People will find any reason to shame you
because they are ashamed of themselves.
Therefore, I have resolved on this day,
the anniversary of my birth—a dawn like any other
in a Queens maternity hospital,
night shift giving over to day, one nurse
remarking on the vast circumference of my infant chest
while Mother wept over my crooked pinkies—
I have resolved to celebrate these hands,
which decoration could never enhance
nor lotion un-line nor lavishly expensive manicure
make passably pretty. Especially now,
with their ridges, divots, and crepe,
so like the potatoes they held, the dirt and the money,
the keys, ink, seeds, bottles, so much
menstrual blood, cum, pussy, tears. Useful,
they were, a comfort as they stroked, with care and without,
striking out or shaping, making, getting,
getting cut, burned, scraped, held. They were
held, my hands. Hands that had always
the look of hands holding out their ticket,
neither next nor the one after next, but Soon, the hands say,
Soon. When I ask how he's feeling, the old man
in Memory Care says, It's like having one left hand
and a second left hand.
Into both of them, then, he rests his face.

ANN FISHER-WIRTH

'Tis a Consummation

When my kids were tiny, all they wanted was to hang on me. Probably my mom felt bereft when she came to visit, when after the first thrill of her presence they would turn to me instead—as now I feel bereft when, after the first thrill, my grandchildren turn to their mothers. There is nothing like the idolatry of the tiny child, that bodily adoration, no way you can be close enough. The hand slipped into yours as you cross the street, the body climbing over yours, sprawling and cuddling as you read a story, the bone-breaking hugs. It's everything, everything.

One day long ago, while my kids and I were visiting, my mom and stepfather drove us to the zoo. Tired, they waited outside while we went to see the animals. When we emerged all sticky with cotton candy and popcorn, they were lying on their sides in the grass, in the dappled sun, softly talking to each other, and I thought, *they are so trusting, as they rest against the earth.* Already the tumor that killed him had begun to grow on his face. *Soon the earth will open and they will slip into their graves.*

My love, my love, we too. Free from the chemicals of embalming, I will be a natural woman, you will be a natural man, and death will wrap us in its cloak, filthy with sticks and feathers. But then at last when our flesh is gone to worms, if we are lucky our bones will mingle, and we will become mud, grasses, mycorrhizae and springtails, bluets in spring, the toothed dogwood tree. Our children will know where in the woods we are buried, and maybe our children's children will plant daffodils on our graves.

EMILY FRANKLIN

Plans

My mother wants her body
turned into human compost
but don't say it like that, say

instead flower bed or more
specific tell everyone she became
moss carpeting the raised trough,

became delosperma, those fire spinner
ice plants each bloom a tiny, breakable
plate opening upon first touch

of light and sleeping as though having been
sung to, *tender Shepard tender Shepard
let me help you count your sheep* let

the body, my mother's body become
all the things she did not—scientist,
visitor to other planets shyly knowing

beings other than people,
gardener, painter of wild irises gone
sideways to the breeze—let her body

be a blanket for my own selfish sorrow
which will grow and return, perennial
forever the way bulbs regrow even after

voles, gray mice, squirrels claw down
into the earth where my mother wants
to become another living, breathing thing

which is to say she wants her body to be
what it has been always to me and who
she became above all else, above

roles and above ankle height, crocuses
and hyacinth, my mother wants to become
or maybe to stay seasonless as sorrow
as green or rot, mother mother mother mother.

KAREN FRIEDLAND

It Recurred

Yes,
this cancer is doing its damndest to kill me,
and it will, eventually.
This is guaranteed.

But right now,
my scrappy, hardy body prevails—

spills words onto pages,
accepts hugs from neighbors,
makes savory dinners,
appreciates fall crickets—

I am living a somehow sweeter life,
here on the precipice,

with a gut full of growing tumors,
on the knife-edge of hope and terror.

At this tender moment,
my death is merely theoretical,
and life is all I'll ever know.

My Body as a Communist Country

Its betrayal totalitarian—
skin dry as parchment

      lit by the slightest brush.
The scent in our

      sheets sets off chimes,
a measure until you

      return.
The minutes I swallow whole.

Castro, you've nothing in Cuba like my desire.

      My body's capitalism,
greedy. It's a slow-jam

in a darkened room
keeping time with a DJ.

      Its lyric, *the blue light of aging shadows*

desire's waking. Ten years from now
      we'll wonder at this

my body's exacting power
      brooking no opposition.

CMARIE FUHRMAN

Dear Body

It was never your fault. It was not how you were dressed, not your fault you developed full breasts and savage hips at a young age, or that your Uncle said, "look at that swing," as you walked in front of him, age 8. Dear Body, it is not your fault that wearing a short skirt puts you in jeopardy, that the brown of your skin puts you in the minds of others that call you exotic, consider you easy. And that because I believed them I spread my dear legs. Dear Legs, I know you wanted to run. Dear Heart, forgive me for trying to fool you. And Body forgive me as we try to forgive Disney for sexualizing Pocahontas, as we forgive whomever perverted the word squaw, invented the ridiculous buckskin mini dress that appears on a tanned body in every single John Wayne western. Dear John Wayne, I forgive you for hating horses, but I don't forgive you using fake Indians to manifest your big screen destiny, in fact, I don't forgive you for using Indians at all to make cowboys and killing iconic, heroic. But I forgive myself for the time when I was twelve and saw you swagger across the TV and thought you were the kind of man I would be safe with, a real man. Dear Real Men, I am thinking about what the term real means, particularly to my body, specifically my blood, wherein lies the DNA of generations of Native women, who now address you, who now charge you with an explanation for the scars of your scalpels and your slurs. If real equals strong and strong equals powerful, by which I mean someone decides what happens to others, then I address you. But without salutation because no salutation is unkind enough to address the decisions your made about our dear bodies. I am talking to you policy makers. I am talking to you George HW Bush. I am pointing my finger at your chest, your dear body, which is still, so far as I know, intact, or at least was when you suggested a bill to congress, which was passed by Richard Nixon, that allowed doctors to remove the uterus, ovaries, womb, ability for Native American women to reproduce. As many as 60,000. Our population fell by 75 percent. I am talking to you and to the America that allowed it. Dear America, I forgive you because, Dear America, we are still here. Still fighting for rights to our bodies for our mothers, our daughters, our sisters. Dear Sisters. Dear Uterus, Dear Womb, Dear legs and hair, and eyes, and breast, and glorious brown skin, and luck of being born Native to a naïve America, the cuts were deep but not fatal. We are still here. Still dear. Dear Body, dear Bodies, dear dear Bodies.

JEANNINE HALL GAILEY

Self-Portrait as a Body Shaped by Illness

My brain forms storm clouds.
My veins run hot and cold.
The idea of weather passes through
my joints, fingers, spine,
tingling with the rain.
Fire burns in the passes,
smoke in my hair. My nails
glitter like lightning. My limbs
are loosened, serpents that refuse to stay still,
my lips too twisted to kiss.
My throat a knotted root.
My two feet untethered, able to float,
tipped to tangle. Take me in your arms,
I will not remain the same—
first one form, then another:
a tree, a lake, a swan, a changeling
that burns its image into the bed.

SONIA GREENFIELD

All the Women I Know Are Writing Post-Roe Poems

about babies we chose not to have so
we could have the babies we did want
or about our almost babies or about preferring
words over babies in the first place—that in
exchange we were allotted time measurable
in units larger than the tiny spoons mothers
come to cherish until we acknowledge how stingy
a trifle of time is, and those spoons tarnish right
in front of our eyes.   Sometimes, before we knew
any better, we would try to save men who were
lodged in the birth canal of perpetual infancy,
and we decided in a rare moment of clarity
we would give them anything but our days
and babies they would have abandoned
anyway, so we're writing
about all of them:
                babies crawling into view
from the shadows with eyes just like their dads'
and dads who couldn't give up the bottle or
who wouldn't wash off the abuse with which
they reek, perfumed by the hands of their own
fathers.   Some women are writing lines tinged
with what could have been—too many maybes
clustered in the margins. The rest of us prefer

not to go there. Instead, we recognize the mists
of wistfulness that barely pull together into
the shapes of babies, then we write those
regrets right back into the cloud.

DAVID GROFF

Days of 1986

My suspect blood.
Dr. Siroty filled a vial
I had to take myself
down the grim avenue
to the Board of Health
in the cold spring evening,
crosswalk after crosswalk
as the sun sidled in.
I saw hundreds of others
like me bearing their blood
but inside their bodies.

The vial—I wanted to pluck it
from my backpack and
prop it on top of a pay phone
or stash it in the trashcan
with the dead Daily News,
wanting no news, not even
good news, knowing news
either way would cleave
me from my brothers.

But I kept taking steps,
the street annoying with life,
the sun incumbent,
the storefronts bloody gold,
until I had to enter

the Board of Health to find
an unguarded tray of vials
and place mine among them,
all of us numbered,
together in our before.

I went back into a city
vital with night, where
no matter my status,
the world would be a blade
so cutting that at times
I could feel I could feel.

My Mother Approves

It was not evening-out jewelry,
not twice-a-year jewelry.
She slept in it. She always said
when she died I would have it
but almost certainly never
pictured me wearing it:
how it would lie an inch
below my beard, in the hollow
between my clavicles,
how the serpentine chain
would catch stray hairs
on my shoulders and neck
and the emerald bright
with its corona of diamond chips
would fill the open collar
of a flannel shirt, over jeans,
brown belt, work boots, and be,
to the right kind of man, a signal—
a traffic light glowing green
at the most vulnerable spot
on my throat. Now in death,
she understands the necklace
was always about drawing the eye
to the flesh: a way to scoop
light from the air, to make
a man want to catch that light
like a snowflake on his tongue.

Yes. That's the word
she's saying to the body
most like her own once was,
briefly incarnating herself
in front of me to straighten
the chain. My mother like
any mother willing her child
to be beautiful: *Yes, it fits
like that, close to your throat.*

JARED HARÉL

Achilles

My brother came down with a defensive
rebound in a body prized and trained
against time, much like Achilles
believed he was invincible
until Paris's arrow torpedoed his heel.
Who plunges into battle
without proper footwear? Nearly forty,
my brother wore low-tops—
heard the hard pop of tendon
as he fell. Here on the sofa, his left leg elevated
beside prescription painkillers
and a bottle of blue Gatorade, I strain to stay
casual. Keep things upbeat. I say,
Did you hear there's one Blockbuster left in America?
or, *Achilles actually died of his wound,*
so by most accounts, you're doing really well.
When that fails to take, I challenge
my brother in *NBA 2K*. We orchestrate
fadeaways, no-look alley-oops—
pixels so intuitive it feels almost true.
But the truth is I don't know
what to do for him. When his best friend,
Patroclus, was killed in battle,
Achilles came out of retirement to avenge
his death—slaughtered Hector,
then dragged his corpse across Troy.
I buy my brother crosswords

and sour gummy worms,
sit through whatever movie he wants to see
as we nurse an ache both sudden
and ancient: these bodies that hold us.
This watching them go.

DENNIS HINRICHSEN

[*lyricism*] [WITH MAY SWENSON AND CECIL THE SPEED DEMON TURTLE]

Body my house
my horse my hound
what will I do
when you are fallen
  —"Question," May Swenson

Hello toyltle
  —Bugs Bunny, "Shell Shocked"

you have to stand naked before the nurse before you stand naked before God—that's what rehab says—the nurse—today—a girl fresh out of community college maybe (where he and I taught) and him—first shower—a grown man with all the sinew and blood squeezed out of him—nearly every strata—how quickly this has happened—naked as that turtle in Looney Tunes—not even a pair of red boxers to keep it PG—just nudity and cotton—care the god (*soapy rag on his back*) erosion the demon—I know that now—but body is animal—the horse—May Swenson said that—the body is engine is mule is hound—brain the rider watching dearest creature die lifting arm so nurse can scrub the pits—*at least the water's warm*—that's what friend thinks muttering haiku and tanka I will read another day—his templebrain facing squarely coming desertdark

CAMILLE HERNANDEZ

Hence this Worn Lament

my shin hasn't been the same since the recession tore intricately woven ligaments   I had once known hope   now I must

relearn existence as a zero sum

product of a generation reminded it can't umbilical cord out of someone else's sin   this is my body   given up to finance an

allergy to idleness   hustling humanity out of our fascia   pity what reconnects us is the discordance of "could be"   darling

I'll feast on your cartilage reference eucharist   make home from cracked bones in invisible hands   your palms are sweating black

pools like pupils dilated for inconstant calmness   there's a story here about how the moon reshined its bull market economy to convince

on our night drenched faces   in turn   we eclipsed our lymphatic tissues for a license to unzip ourselves   inflation's next casualty

KAREN HILDEBRAND

Secretly, I Named a Flower for You

> *Child. My blood at night full of your dreams.*
> —Muriel Rukeyser, "nine poems (for the unborn child)"

Child. Little cutting
little bud, my blood.
Not your fault
the way jasmine blooms
at night. Not your fault
the fists of mint that
smother the beds.

Forgive me, child
not child, who I yanked
out as if bindweed.
Secretly, I call you
Hyssop and sip your
fragrance in my sleep.

EMILY HOCKADAY

The Heart Grows Full of Weeds

Shepherd's purse, dandelion, sorrel. Too many root in the soft and vulnerable places for me to safely excise them. To tug on the stalks would dislodge the buried past, the lungs, my muscles and ligaments. We all want to survive and sometimes that means propagating past the point of sense. The shepherd's purse shatters, and seeds take to the wind. My cardiologist says, of my chest cavity: *there are so many organs packed together in there.* He's not worried about the skipped beats or the pounding. I tend to myself when no one else will. I tend to overthink. *Honeybees aren't picky*, says the local beekeeper. They thrive on clover and dandelion and violets. The ordinary plants that grow between sidewalks and cardiac tissue. The stalwart vegetation that fills the holes in your memory or your days or your lawn.

ANDREA HOLLANDER

Wound

When you asked if I wanted to see
and I said yes, you opened your robe,
lifted off the gauze, and exposed
a barbed wire fence cut
through a field of snow.
The snow wasn't white exactly
but used or forgotten, the air
hardened by winter so that
to breathe was to choke.
And along its black length
that separated into two
your past and your future,
that fence was streaked
with indecipherable detritus
as though some small animal
had been dragged from its life into it
and died there, its clots of fur
still frozen in the barb.
This is your chest, I told myself,
not some deserted pasture
flattened by winter over
what is lost or missing.
I should have closed my eyes
or pictured the ocean instead.
Twenty-seven years after your death
I still can't turn away. I shut my eyes

and see your chest stitched closed.
If only snow were the only way
to know such cold.

JP HOWARD

in this house

we raise our voices
we are raising up black boys in this house
in this house, some days our voices stay raised high
other nights we are soft whispers
black boys are becoming black men in this house
in this house black boys blossom
black boys bloom
black boys cry or laugh
black boys be brilliant in this house
this is a black boys house filled with love
we don't let fear into this house
we know fear intimately,
but we don't let it enter these doors
this is a safe house for black boys becoming black men
this is a safe house for black men who were once black boys
this is our house and these are our suns.

JESSICA JACOBS

Sex, Suddenly, Everywhere

In shop class, that redhead with the jumpsuit zippered
from throat to crotch, trilling, *Boys,*

don't touch my zipper, until they trailed her like goslings, transfixed
by the shiny metal pull. The couple caught

naked in the science building bathroom. Backhand
whispers of *But I wouldn't even take my shoes off in there!* And how many

eighth-grade dance parties in a country club boathouse, some girl
in the corner crying about some boy, some boy nervously plucking

the wales of his corduroys, waves lapping—unheard but always lapping—
as I got freaked by the Pagan twins to a *Boys II Men* slow jam.

Confused girl meshed between two confused brothers, I tried not to stare
at the girls I wished against me instead.

∞
And every day those hallways: crowded cattle shoots, musked up
clusters of young bodies, slap of sandals, snap of bra straps, high sweet
stench of mall-bought perfume. My nose to the back of another girl's

neck, close enough to see a single strand, escaped, curling beneath
her collar, the gym class dampness between her shoulder blades. Sometimes
it was all I could do to keep my clothes on. To keep from moaning

aloud. Once a bucket—an occasional, embarrassing slosh over the top
if jostled—now a sieve, desire leaking from every pore. Which is why
I tried so hard to be harder. To use the world as my whetstone, sharpening

myself against each day. My body cried out for armor. Big boned,
broad shouldered, I was built for it: forced into a dress with shoulder pads,
I was the 90s' littlest linebacker. So I began to run, clanking

like a tank around cul-de-sacs. Began to climb, building biceps
strong enough to stiff-arm the world away. Even my heart grew
heavy, grew into one more thing to carry.

MARA JEBSEN

Deep Water Women

After the movie, the matinee
        subway back to Brooklyn, windowscene
panels, aluminum, plastic, bluish
           tile, february, melancholy.

Melissa Mcarthy played a mean-sad woman
of uncompromising choices and literary devotions
       lurid, they said her life was
a lurid literary life
       whiskey, catpoop, flies
nyc winters,
       I am beside the side stitching—
the stuffing of that life tumbles at
       mine.

Half my hair is already white
       I am at Hoyt street.

Someone wild entered the car
             and knocked trash off the seat
     with her foot
   her hair is mermaid hair
           and she is middle-aged.

We fit in the slot
       the engineered tunnels.

I will write a poem called
      deep water women
    in which time stops outside the water
      and no one in the city can age or progress
until the old mermaids have finished their swim.
          Doesn't it feel good
      to near your house
          your own seawater washing your organs
      your stars your friends in your mind like a crown all around
your own tongue lolling
      cooing any song
with your fine mermaid mouth.

MELISSA FITE JOHNSON

Hereditary

At a funeral, an old woman asks what's wrong.
I'm furious. My brother just says what's wrong,

cerebral palsy. He balances as best he can.
He trails behind. I link my arm through his,

carry his plate to the table, but
don't make a big deal. I'd do it for anyone.

His biological mother died giving birth.
He didn't get enough oxygen.

The stress he must've felt just becoming.
What we pass on, even without shared blood.

Our father trailed behind after his strokes.
I linked my arm through his. I carried his plate.

PATRICIA SPEARS JONES

Dancer

The man with the black feather tattoo pares this space
Between fantasy and the memory of a man's carved
Torso, designed for stroking and celebration.

Today the sun's brightness is like that lover's kiss,
Wonderful in the present and greater in memory.

A memory that brings me back to that black feather's
Flutter. Stars dazzle in some other part of this world
Where the sun has set and the moon illuminates
Swans diving into voluminous waters.

JEN KARETNICK

On our 31st wedding anniversary, I discover my heart has hardened,

its cave-like passageways half-occluded
with helictites that catch the blood flow
in their corkscrews. I am rock, rock, steadied;

in kidney lobes, calcium has marbled
every so often to bowl itself through
cave-like passageways which, half-occluded,

spill out scarlet protests, undiluted.
Stones inch out from salivary glands, too:
fragile corkscrews. I am rock, rock, steadied,

particles gathering in joints, crystallized.
My body collects quartz but not for show,
its cave-like passageways half-occluded,

redirecting grit to whirlpool, eddied.
Pan me for gold and find pebbles to throw,
plane, and corkscrew: rock, rock, unsteadied.

Still, with amethyst glint, geoded,
I'll break open to the chisel of you.
My cave-like passageways half-occluded—
not yet screwed—I'm rocked by rocks, am steadied.

MEG KEARNEY

Duckling, Swan

Before I was born I was biggest of the clutch, already a burden
and slow to hatch. When at last I smashed my way into this world,
my mother's tongue unfurled a hiss, siblings snickered and jeered.
Who could love an ugly girl, smothered in egg wax, gray as the curl in
a drowned man's lip? Even cleaned up my down was ash. I was the art
of my mother's mistake, the ache in her dinosaur heart. I was the winter,
the ice-over early, no fish in the pond and the hunter's sure shot. I had
nowhere to go when they drove me out, but I went like something dead
in coyote's mouth. Like something a cat mauled then tossed about.
I starved through the full moons. Slept in the snow. But by spring a lake
was aglow with my gleaming—in spring I returned and blinded them all.

HYEJUNG KOOK

Quick

As in the brown fox which jumps
over the lazy dog, as in cut to the quick,
the living, alive, from Anglo-Saxon *cwic*,
as in *Enoch cwic gewit mid cyning engla*,
Enoch departed alive with the king of angels,
as in *The Quick and the Dead*, the movie
starring Sharon Stone as a gunslinger, the phrase
from Tyndale's translation of the New Testament,
as in quickening—no, not *Highlander*,
that's the Quickening, with a capital Q
and immortals and beheadings and
lightning special effects—I'm talking about
the first stirrings of movement
an expectant mother feels in her belly,
the faintest flutters like butterflies,
like fish swimming, or less bucolically,
often confused with gas, which some feel
as early as thirteen weeks but not I,
with my anterior placenta muffling
my firstborn's movements, not I, who after
two losses, wondered every day, is it/he/she
alive? Is the third time the charm? Sometimes I felt
my every breath was a silent invocation,
wanting so desperately, yet now I can't remember when
I felt it, like bubbles drifting, inner iridescence,
like hope expanding, then disappearing. I don't know
if I will feel it again, but I remember it now

because my secondborn is sleeping curved
against my bared breast, and one hand rests
on my cheek, and dreaming, her fingers are
tapping a barely felt pattern against my skin,
faint and lovely and alive, quick, in this moment
she is alive, I am alive, I feel the electric charge
in us, brief, improbable, like lightning striking twice.

MICHAEL LALLY

I Meant To

I meant to put those
sixty-three names
and email addresses
in the BCC blind copy
space, not the CC
copy space. I meant to

send it to him, not her.
I meant to swallow not
drool, on the computer,
my lap, your sleeve, my
arm, the floor, that first
edition, in the drawer.

I meant to walk and
move with that feline
grace someone once
said I had, not wobble
and stagger like an
old wino. I meant to

hit the "y" not the "t"
the "h" not the "g"
the "b" not the "v",
return not send,
amends not amen.
I meant to stand up

straight not bend, to
sit upright not slouch,
to not fall down and
get stuck between the
couch and a hot pipe
that burned my back

like the prolonged
sting of a fierce slap.
I meant to stay twenty-
nine or forty-nine, not
be seventy-nine turn-
ing eighty in May this

way, drooling and
stumbling and un-
able to make a fist
with my right hand
or grasp a utensil in
the proper way but

instead need foam
additions to the
handles for my one
or two fingers that
can still curl without
help. I meant to be

the exception to
obviously aging or
a long gone legend
by now not a bent
over drooling old
man who still often

feels like a woman
inside but I'll accept
what I'm left with for
as long as I can and
still be grateful for all
that I've been and am.

LANCE LARSEN

Quail Egg

While watering I found it under the Ponderosa pine,
a stray egg, already cold, dropped by a stray

hen in a hurry for better cover. A thing like that
you have to save, but my PJs had no pockets,

so I polished it on my sleeve and popped it
into the wet pouch of my mouth for safe keeping.

Its shell tasted like calcium, like sun, which is to say
like nothing at all. I moved that oval prayer

cheek to cheek, and even the names of my hostas—
Stained Glass, Blue Angel, Fire and Ice—

seemed to bear witness to a new magnetic north.
Was the egg fertilized? Should I call it a compass,

cook it in bacon fat? I felt old as an alderman,
young as rain. And for a moment, oppositions

held: tame/feral, inside/outside, slug/sky.
Then Jacqui called from the kitchen for me

to grab a ripe peach or two, and the world wrinkled.
I answered in a nothing voice, like the groggy man

she'd kissed awake at dawn, but already I could taste
funerals on my tongue, wings budding at my back.

VIOLA LEE

Mixtape

You made it the summer you left home. It seems irrelevant now
since you can't seem to find a working tape player — the ones
in the thrift shops are picked over again and in the antique stores
all of them are too vintage. But how you remember hearing
those songs or making one in return to sustain a memory.
Something those songs do to the body whenever you hear them.
You never really can forget once they have been memorized.
How they live in the body and become concrete. How they waken
each cell and become a truth you protect. It is human to want
to keep something. It is human when a body knows and can not let go.

EUGENIA LEIGH

Gold

I've become
the kind of creature who, on Sundays,
fills seven small boxes with a bevy of pills

to stick it out another week.
When will I be fixed enough
to hear my kid scream without tearing

my father's phantom hands off me?
How do demons, decades gone now,
still ravage me? Tell me

I am not the thing
my child will have to survive.
Tell me

the mob I inherited will not touch
my son. Yes, the cavalcade
of all that's tried to kill me

may forever raid my brain, but know
this: in my mother's first language,
the word for *fracture*, for *crack*,

is the same as the word for *gold*.
Every Thursday for twenty-one months
before my son was born,

a doctor trained me to put the gun down
and write.　　　　　I understand
I am one of the lucky ones.

REBECCA LINDENBERG

The Splendid Body

The splendid body is meat, flexor
and flesh pumping, pulling, anti-
gravity maverick just standing
upright all over museums and
in line for the bus and in the laundry
aisle where it's just standing there
smelling all the detergent like
it's no big deal. So what if a couple
of its squishy parts are suspended
within, like beach-bungled jellyfish
in a shelved jar, not doing anything?
Nothing on this side of the quantum
tunnel is perfect. The splendid body,
though, is splendid in the way
it keeps its steamy blood in, no matter
how bad it blushes. And splendid
in how it opens its mouth and
these invisible vibrations come
rippling out—if you put your wrist
right up to it when that happens
it feels somewhat like the feet
of many bees. The splendid body
loves the juniper smell of gin, loves
the warmth of printer-fresh paper,
and the sound fallen leaves make
under the wheel of a turning car.
If you touch it between the legs,

the splendid body will quicken
like bubbles in a just-on teakettle.
It knows it can't exist forever, so
it's collecting as many flavors as it can—
saffron, rainwater, fish-skin, chive.
Do not distract it from its purpose,
which is to feel everything it can find.

MATTHEW LIPPMAN

The Treasure of the Silence after the Hard Scrabble Lurch and Lunge for Love

I want to start with the word *treasure*.
My father was a treasure.
He wasn't really a box of gold bullion or anything like that,
big jade jewels, *forgetaboutit*.
He just floated through the house.
Sometimes he'd be there in the attic
putting insulation between the boards.
Other times he'd be at the dinner table but he wasn't at the dinner table.
Where are you, man? I'd think.
I never wondered what he said to my mother
when they shut their bedroom door.
What was going on in there?
What goes on in any room with any closed doors?
Plans for war?
Secret silences?
Straight up fucking or up straight watching television?
There was a lot of television watching in my house
and I'm sure, not a lot of fucking,
except when I turned 17 and then, look out.
The treasure of the teenage body.
The treasure of the silence after the hard scrabble lurch and lunge for love.
What I knew about lovemaking I knew my father did not.
He was a treasure of absence and had no idea he had a body.
Today I wheeled his atrophied frame up 71st street towards 1st.

He's gone now, his mind,
but that did not stop him from saying hello to everyone who walked
    by, like a toddler,
like a mayor.
He wore an orange cap and remembered the bad barbeque joint on the
    corner.
He said, "Let's eat there, what a gift."
He meant being outside—
the treasure of air and wind and pigeon shit and taxi cab holler.
We sat there, he in his wheelchair, me in my sweatshirt,
and downed plates of fried chicken, fries, okra, and cornbread.
I sat and watched his eyes and wondered what was behind them,
glazed and blank and gone.
What a treasure dementia is.
What a blessing to be with him in the absence of his mind
like it doesn't matter where he was in his gluttony and spittle.
Watching him go at the breast, wing, the drumstick,
like he'd never tasted anything that good before, ever,
was the biggest haul a son could ask for. To be there at the moment
when they smash the safe open and you realize there's nothing inside.

MARGAREE LITTLE

Bridle

Talking to you in the kitchen, in the morning,
I shake my head in the gesture of a horse,
trying to toss off the rope around its neck.

It's not a phantom limb, but I can feel her hands there,
as though I'm still her little sister
to pull up short or to send forward,

hooves clacking like teeth on the road.
In the dreams, the me that betrays you
is her, or is like her: I too can make my way

without feeling. Then something else comes to,
remembers that you exist, it's you I'm looking for.
So what is the voice that says, now,

it would be better if she had actually killed me?
What part of her did she leave in me,
so that, without direction, I'd follow her orders—

I know them so well, it's hard to explain them.
When I tried, last night, when I said,
she is someone who doesn't have empathy,

she raped me, I had already left my body,
leaving this ludicrous shaking in the chair.

MIA AYUMI MALHOTRA

On Memory

with lines from Sarah Manguso

Today I am thinking about the mind's relationship to time, and how my daughters are old enough now that there are things they do not remember.

In other words, they have acquired the ability to forget.

In conversation, I find myself saying, *when you were a baby* and *when you were little*, and the look they give me—

It's as though I'm telling them about someone else's life. Which, in a way, I am.

The hours spent in half-sleep, before they knew their hands were their own—watched them drift, of their own volition, in front of their unrecognizing faces.

How it had felt to be wordless, completely of the physical world—that even before my body was an instrument for language it had been an instrument for memory.

You were blue, I say. *The umbilical cord was wrapped around your neck. They took you away, and then they brought you back.*

Her face fills with questions, like water running into a glass. *Why did they take me away? Where did I go? How long until they brought me back?*

With this telling, I am weaving her an origin story—one, I realize, in which I am incidental.

Her dark, rabbity eyes as she lay on my breast, rosy and womb-shaped.

Birth work, the doula reminds me, *is a lifelong process.* I weep to hold these memories, charged with the responsibility of remembering what she does not.

Each drawn-out day and fractured, contraction-gutted night. My belly, a luminous bulge that torqued this way, then that.

How each child, obstructed in some way—one by the entanglement of the umbilical cord, the other by a thick, unforgiving cuff of scar tissue—emerged, roaring with light.

Then the moments after. My belly draped slackly as I stood to pee.

Moments worth remembering, though in recalling them, I risk altering them. Episodic memory, a tricky, shape-shifting thing.

The least contaminated memory might exist in the brain of a patient with amnesia—in the brain of someone who cannot contaminate it by remembering it.

The perfect memory, forged in the newborn's mind, before she knows enough to forget. The tug of soft palate against nipple. The first swallow, followed by the next, that reflex that leads to life.

A kind of grace, that she does not remember this moment enough to lose it.

CHRISTINE MALVASI

S.A.F.E.
    for J

They called the kit a kit
    to reassure you they had steps

        1-2-3 instructions
They asked you to reassemble

the night: first this, then that?
    So you talked about a beard of moss,
the tops of trees

        Strong, they shook their heads
   to shake you out of yourself,

     said, *now now*, and slowly
passed swabs

underneath your nails

Afterwards, you said
    you could move things

       The green shirt
you turned into a bird

flying away
   You dusted with feathers

you were not touching,
       said that every evening

you made larkspurs and spiders bloom
   from your belly

       to silence the men in the backyard
who cried like wild cats

You sang high notes loudly

The wine glass in shards

      on the bedroom floor
You blamed the power

of your eyes

CYNTHIA MANICK

Dear Future Body (Keep Your Skin Thickk)

Yesterday my legs were propped
in stirrups as the gyno said,
You should go on The Biggest Loser.
I heard cities at the skull base
stuttering over each other,
vine and vowels *of your rolls*
and the *garden under your chin*.
The implied real estate of—
don't you want to be beautiful?
We have known the trap
of nameless and hungry
BMI indexes.
Dear God and sample-size fashion,
I escape and get caught
in the same geography again and again,
unmade and remade.
I forget I am more than a house
of great bones,
of Vaseline and Werther's Originals.
The Caucasity of a wellmeaning
she has such a pretty face.
I'm writing to tell you about
a type of war,
people carving the cavalry horses
to survive
the outline of social media
models and how many

calories is this bottle of air?
What else can we eliminate?
I always thought the planet Pluto
was a Black girl,
now downgraded and mostly out.
Dear Future Body,
take a break today.
Tell me—how are your kisses?
Sometimes they give birth to promises,
a season in the word,
oil and oxygen at the ready.
Are you someone's night bloom?
Remember to trace what remains,
the prayers your mouth learns.
I want us living, not just alive.

FRED MARCHANT

the burning road

———

the teacher draws a line on the black board and urges us to stare at it
until our eyes begin to water and sting
until the line starts to waver
until we are not so sure it is only a line
the teacher says the line is the world
now close your eyes and erase that line
the goal is to forget it ever existed
tell us what you see in the darkness left behind
speak without guile, says the teacher, or fear of rebuke
thus i announce the world is burning
this that has come to me is neither dream nor delusion
i see tree-tall rushes on fire, both sides of the road
flame-arms joining together high up
a flailing arch we have to pass under
a red yellow darkness at the heart of it
this is birth i first think, no this is death, no
this is the day we met, no
this is how one of us will have to leave first, no
this is how the other will have to follow, no
this is the low-level roar that cuts through everything
yes a messenger has come to tell us why we are here
yes and why we must pass through this
yes through that which consumes what it was made of
this?

———

yes

JENNIFER MARTELLI

By August

they're already hanging witch
dolls from the eaves and the ledges
of the homes in Salem

and from the windows of shops where I buy
local goods: waxy combs, balms,
and a small owl

candle with a long wick. A dragonfly
leads me past a hedgerow
of autumn olives. August

yields her sun low, lower,
lower each day. I curve
into the fall, lick the parts that hurt

most, my wounded willow bark, my
animal skin. Last night, in a dream, this:
I cradled a corn cob doll to me,

urged it to nurse the nothing that's left,
became less sad, less of a conduit.
Can I deconstruct an asexual life

and call this home? Can I not allow
touch and still love?
Come morning, I pondered the exclusion

of queen bees in fall. My hair
was a willow nest of cold blue eggs
and I could smell the wine from the small

apples that fell, rotten and bruised,
to the ground below my window.
All night, I'd simmered on low

shimmery citrus rinds—
a tea I could drink, a balm
boiled down. Come, mourning, take

the inch of light: orbit wider farther
away. My back arcs into place. Out back,
tomatoes choke, thick on their vines. At last,

the pepper plants have turned deep purple. Fall
curves here, a pelted thing, amber.
You have to see it, the light.

GAIL MARTIN

Coming Back Body

Here, the body that collapses like butter in sun. The futile body waxing and shattering in a minor key, the stooped body leaning hard toward another surgery. The reined-in body that groans rising from a chair, fighter pilot body born again as razor blades and pop cans. Fencepost body, brittlebush body. The body awake at 3, beaded with salt, salt crunchy around swollen eyes. The limping body, the slow-motion body, the ruptured body with sutured hips, a purple gash that means maybe. Tears in the shower that mean captivity, that mean heal me, grotesque puckers on each side that suggest the unseen body, buried body, I think the soul. Here is the beat-up body, the deconstructed, dislocated body, here is the body coming to terms, cast-off body, body without its own parts. Don't try to pretty it. The body that rains bees. The betraying body, the bonegrief body. Bring me the plumed body, transformed body, flash body playing banjo, the body tap dancing. Show me the flowering body, the standing up body, the no-one-can-witness-this-and-be-unmoved body. The sugared body, barefoot body, honeyed body, body that swaggers, body that soars, body that flourishes, sweet-talking body, charming itself back home.

TRAPETA B. MAYSON

Sweet Mornings

Rise before the world begins to stir
Before the busyness of its hive
Swarms, stings, and swells you

Your skin that puckers and bristles at every slight
And goosebumps with angst and anxieties
Let it be stroked and shined
Let it be oiled like warriors marching into battle
So slick that everything hurled at it will slide

Your heart that is a raw raw thing
That hardly grieves before another avalanche
Blows through its delicate chambers
Let it be pumped and pumped with rememberings
Of mother and brother and the friend who left you
Shout down into its red clenched walls, beat, beat

Your body that betrays
With flesh over growing in once taut places
Do not be tempted to bruise it too
Telling it that it's ugly and useless and unworthy
Douse it in lullabies to your hearty bones
And slow drag with your spreading supple terrain
Your well traveled land, your magical canvas
Drape yourself in full regalia and flow, flow

Relish in the quiet hours, *love*
Before the day announces itself
You, *dear human*
Prep yourself for what lies ahead
Greet it so it knows you're alive
Open your hands to catch your portion
Part your mouth to swallow it all
You, lone conductor of your life
Let yourself be serenaded by stillness
By the soft pulsing music of
Your sweet mornings

CAITLIN GRACE MCDONNELL

Portrait at 52

My right shoulder,
an outline of pain.
Bone on bone after
accidents, carrying
smaller bodies; letting
heads rest in the recesses.
I take my bag off to rest
at the airport by a window,
less visible than in my shiny-
haired youth, I can watch
the slow loading and unloading
with fuller eyes. Crown of hair
now lit with strips of white.
I love to dance, and dancing
now is always partly working
out the knots. My father slamming
doors folded beneath my shoulder
blade. The friend who betrayed
me in the hardness of my jaw.
The small muscles in my arms
could still lift my daughter
out of danger even now
that she is taller than me.
Heavy lids over my dark
grey blue eyes. I finally
look like I feel, like someone
who has been through

something. Constellation
of freckles on my leg
the same for half a century
like the map of the heavens.

LYNN MCGEE

This Is It

Your sternum,
where I rested my head those years
we shared a bed,
has been cracked like a lobster claw,
and a jigsaw in the surgeon's hand
flicks its razor tongue—
Behold the pericardium,
milky veil that guards
your fist of a heart,
finally loosening its grip.
This morning
in a southern state saturated
in sunshine and free
of helmet laws, a young man
was mangled beyond repair,
but his strong heart hunkered down
in its cave, was gently pried out
like a barnacle
and his gift, in its yellow
cushion of fat, was packed in ice,
flown north
and rolled with expert haste
to the West Side of Manhattan
where you sat up in bed dialing
the call that buzzed
in my backpack—you text me,
too: *This is it,*

and by nightfall, surgeons stitch
the pulsing muscle of a stranger
into the cavity of your chest,
atrium to atrium, vein to vein,
and your blood finds
its new hub, and passes
through.

ERIKA MEITNER

Touch Cave

I am no bird but
I would like someone
to cradle me the way
a nest nestles its eggs
& this airport bathroom
stall almost comes
through. In the new
terminal everyone
on my flight waited
for a shuttle to Gate D
because our good
fortune at arriving
somewhere like Gate
48, spit-shined & well-
designed, couldn't
last. I didn't see you
on this island or in
a hotel bed or on a
train so I walked
the wet streets.
I went to a bar
where they served
drinks with names
like Wakeup Call &
Bark at the Moon.
I touched myself
the way a person

presses a button
on a soda machine
that isn't working—
not the way you
sweep the return
with one finger for
someone else's left-
behind change—
I'm talking after you
put your dollar in.
You have a lot
going on. We are
all beholden to
something. Every-
one is so tired.
Everyone is buffeted
by the wind. No matter
where I sit on this jet,
I am over the wing.

JENNIFER MILITELLO

Odaxelagnia

When I sink my teeth into you,
there is a taste, a satisfaction, the start
of a match, the catch in your throat.
We are rich with the exhilarations
of our blood, we are rich with our
print-blackened roots, like the crowns
of my teeth in you cracked like dirt,
enamel-fragile and eggshell-veined. I sink
my teeth and they knit your history
a coat. I shut the cold like a tap
and lean like a trunk and we unravel
as though thread and when we fall,
the quiet is like a feather, like
a bough. It was a God I held
in the trap of my mouth, in you,
my rabbit gone limp, my bite
at your neck and me tasting fur
like wind and me tasting the scent
of you melted as wax. A wick lit,
it was my path, it was a desire
to solidify and start. At the front.
At the back. In the lip. At its cry.
No dry soul unsickened yet. I sink
my teeth. I notch your depth. I prove
it has terror, an Atlantic I've wept.

SAMANTHA MOE

I can't see you by the shore anymore but I pretend you're still here/ we make dinner for our children

There are fish and daughters, salt and a regretful
sea, unfair the wildlife doesn't care about me and
what do you want to do about dinner, should we
tell the daughters to give up their sea bass and perch
should we sun the fish or place them in shady buckets
is your favorite color still blue, do you know of alligator
in the fields, their mouths opened waiting for rain, you
were smoking in the back door, ignoring me, obsessing
again over the harbor, she's not coming back, left you
with me and them, I've also said goodbye to my husband
could be your partner or cluster, if you wanted, a fry
or broken-down car, the ring on your finger, thick as jam
jars within which we once placed fins, starved starfish
found crusty on the shore, jam jars with milk and small
minnows with small mouths, white peaches and ombre
peaches, you don't want me to help you anymore, you
want the daughters to tie your hair with tendons, I see
your body most nights, out with lanterns looking for
your wife, likely eaten by the sea, wish I could keep
you company but these days I barely keep my mind
local, I am a freshwater chicken, I am a terrible catch,
I channel rivers into static, pretend I'm sleeping when
you, soft-footed, drape a blanket over my body, this
couch is lonely, our love will never be in season, but

the next morning you wake like nothing happened,
hair still with half-broken blood, asking me if I'll help
grab tomato buckets, open clams, make her stew.

FIA MONTERO

Diastasis Recti Abdominis

is the vertical   separation   of the anterior
abdominal wall   along the *linea alba*.
embryonic swell   stretches apart the muscles,
splitting them open   like an overripe peach.
my children recall   this anatomical rending
as they pat the valley   running down my abdomen,
bury their marzipan   faces in the window of me.
i like to imagine they   made the gap with intention.
left a keyhole to climb   back inside,
play hide-and-seek   among familiar viscera.
but there is no room   to wedge two wiry bodies
into this snug home.   my belly is full of ghosts
weaving wet   shadows, discarded
membranes.

CARIDAD MORO-GRONLIER

To the Childhood Friend who Shrugged when *Roe vs Wade* was Overturned because She Claimed to Have No Skin Left in the Game

You were the girl who leaned
against the locked door
of a McDonald's bathroom stall,
halfway through a double shift
you picked up to buy a pregnancy
test you couldn't afford after tuition
and rent, your boyfriend a light switch—
off and on and off again.

He didn't have a job and your terror
was no small thing. You knew
too much about going it alone,
living check to check, trying to break
a mold too slight to contain the want
for a life unlike your mother's—beholden
to her husband, your father, a cruel supervisor
at the girdle factory, duty bound, strapped
to a kid-ruled life that stopped being
her own long before it ever began.

Your brown polyester uniform pooled
on the floor, quivered with the current
of your trembling. And even though

the tiny window on that plastic stick
never did turn pink, we had a plan,
in case it did. We had choices then,
choices that did not include a bassinette.

Although I had not yet found myself
in the same predicament, I never did forget
how cold your hands were as we waited
at the sink. I held them in my own,
kept you warm with my very skin.

MARY MORRIS

Appointment with Dr. Siegel

Across the neurosurgeon's massive desk
sits a small pot with a brain cactus.

Maybe it's not funny. I pretend I don't see it.
He speaks of a ten-hour surgery

as if it storms today, yet tomorrow
we set sail for sunny Grenada.

Sometimes tools resemble weapons.
So I departed that office within

a concrete steel obelisk of a medical spire
in the boom-box of Spanish Harlem

where I met the A train, left with the decision
of whether to be blinded and paralyzed

by an operation that would obliterate
the malformation—or take my chances.

I was a new mother.
My blouse flowered with milk.

ALICIA REBECCA MYERS

Giving Birth May Alter a Mother's Bones

It isn't the depletion of calcium and phosphorus that leaves me
unable to stand at times but the world. My liver is a river bed,
my uterus a planetary nebula. My lungs have become
secondary to your survival. When I try to sleep, I feel my marrow
weeping. What swaths of toxic stew will you inherit? There is nothing
I wouldn't offer up on my platelets if it meant you might
not suffer. Right now, sick on the couch
watching walkthroughs, you can't possibly know the extent
of my changed pancreas or that my brain was refashioned into
a crouching lioness when you were born. I only recognize
my heart because you carry it.

RACHEL NEVE-MIDBAR

Somewhere Within

> *it was common that women were treated for nymphomania, hysteria and any "female" imbalance by being bled with leeches on their vulva and perineum.*
> —Gronemen, *Nymphomania: A History*

Perhaps the Dr. was called late, late into the night, nightly, late
and called again, his black bag crammed with the clink of leeches,

jars lined up to suck her selfhood yet again, set like moss across her vulva,
the pink flesh of her mind never condensed, engorged in spider veins

sprung free. Perhaps, she wants to know all of it. Perhaps. Perhaps
they call her witch, they call her hysteric; perhaps, she wants to know:

do leeches drink well from her disease? O the curious leech who escapes
his fate to swim within, enter her blood-yolk—here her marriage bed:
    long—ing

clot-remorse; what is the will of a willful barnacle? To attach: the sides
    of her womb
finally filling, an embryo of selfsuck-blood to grow fast and fat, round

like days and nights alive; o, sponge, o, shudder—to convulse this way.
    Yes—
they call her witch, her unwashed hair, yes, her spiral eyes,

yes, they call her hysteric, bleeding the parts impacted, the parts expended,
yes—used, though never released—o, the packing: her words finally
    drowned

to the density of an ignited chain reaction, wildfire release—child child finally—leech-child born to shatter, mosquito-like, in her arms.

JOSHUA NGUYEN

After I Was Mistaken for the Stripper While Delivering Barbeque to an All-White Bachelorette Party

i.

    If I had a stripper name, it would be *pork loins*. Marinated in my mother's seasoning, I am mostly bone, but my butt is meaty. My neck is long, but you can still love me if you want to brisket. In the eventual end, it will be my *own* doing. If I had a dollar bill for every human who wanted to see me naked . . . I would still be paying loans back. "Being wanted" was never simmered. I am the lamb's wool & the wolf crying beneath thin skin. Lick between my ribs. Enriched blandness. I am best served with oyster sauce.

ii.
& there I stood
a bag of meat
head in the crosshairs
unknown terrain
door closing behind
young deer in the trenches
stay motionless
don't make the first move
kindled fire
feet too warm
apple between the teeth
arrow pointed to the naval
knives & forks

& forks & stomachs
lack of fat
sucked bones
upside down
blood draining
unconsciousness
serpent at my throat
boiling rice
serpent in my throat
not clean
serpent down my throat

iii.
Is this what being a sacrifice smells like?
Twenty-six jewel-studded cowboy boots circle me,
tongues glistening in the spur of heat.

REBECCA HART OLANDER

Anniversary

Do you wonder how I'm getting along
without you? I'm still here, clearing

your calendar, donating your clothes,
taking a scythe to your future.

I'm felled. On the path alone. Not by myself,
but unaccompanied. So long, girlfriend,

who did my braids, my mascara.
Pulled that hair I didn't see under my chin.

It's about the body, how I loved you,
about our unshaven legs and the silver

in our hair. How I can find pleasure in mine,
or not. How you could, or not, in yours.

We *get* each other, or *got*, but *get* feels
less worn, less like a dissolving

groove on a record, or forgetting the lyrics
we belted together in your car.

Pacing an icicled route, animal bones
mark the trail. Today is the same day again

as the day you died. Your face was all
I will ever need to know of cheekbones.

Can't we hang out again
in that follow-the-hours way,

like at Old Navy trying on jeans?
I miss when I'd call and you'd answer.

LISA OLSTEIN

The Spell

The lover who punished me—
The sea wasp that stung me—

The mold that bloomed behind the walls that housed me—
The evil eye cast by a rival to expel me—

The love gold as any honey hived around me—
The pills I took—

The pills I didn't take—
The doctors, the needles, the vials, the scripts—

The whirring—
The silence—

The sputtering engines of my cells—

The years—
The spell I want to cast across them—

ALIXEN PHAM

It Happens All the Time on the Serengeti

A large crow calls to her assassins
from my sycamore tree, the sound a serrated
knife sawing my ears. Seven ebony hunters

spiral down to the ground. A squirrel's body
lies crushed. Crimson seeps from mouth and eyes,
mats brown fur, stains the air metallic.

The blood is bright as the velvet dress I remember
wearing at five during Christmas, bright as Santa's suit
during my first picture with him. My mother left

me by his side so Father could take a picture of us.
My eyes—dark and far away like this dead mammal—
willed my father to see the heft of Santa's hand

on my bottom, how I sucked darkness down my stomach—
the same way I did years later when a lover said:
Girls like it when I do this.

His hands squeezed my throat like a toothpaste tube.
My tongue silent as he took honey from me.

The crows waddle to the carcass, heads
cocking like guns. They pounce, hammering
a violent song—

the meat of my body rocks with each blow.

When they are done, a Rorschach test
leers at me.

I bury the leftover in the earth.
No flower to mark the location.
No eulogy to commemorate the memory.

Trusting nature to reclaim
what is broken.

MAYA PINDYCK

Addendum

The day we lost the baby is the only day
I've seen you faint & piss yourself & I had
to laugh because blood & loss are nothing
new to a woman & I remembered
the story of adolescent you poking
your finger inside a spinning fan
that sliced off its tip, as it should, & how
you fainted, you tell me, recounting the tale
while fluttering your hands in invisible satin
gloves, signaling a fragile woman—Victorian?—
who can't take the heat—after I released
our dead son into the doctor's hands,
we met my mother for burgers & beers & you
told us everything you saw, what I could not
see from my position facing the ceiling
& your face by our hanging coats & months
later I read Thich Nhat Hanh on death
as a continuum & I believe him
so where is our son?

IAIN HALEY POLLOCK

All the Possible Bodies

My alcoholic grandfather couldn't hold his money
& passed a bad check. Hampton / Virginia / after *Brown
v. Board* but before Selma's Bloody Sunday. After
my grandmother died but before he moved the family
North / back to the town of his birth. My mother saw
her father cuffed & dragged from the house. The next
day / by some miracle she never understood /
he came home.
                Had he looked at the officers wrong /
acted wrong / spoken wrong / been too familiar / been
a few inches taller / been deeper voiced or darker skinned
& for this had he caught a knee that night to the neck
& not returned / perhaps my mother / needing to stay home
& raise Aunt Joan & Uncle Keith / would have skipped
college. Had she skipped college / perhaps she would not
have gone for a Ph.D. Had she not gone for a Ph.D. /
perhaps she would not have met my father. Had she
not met my father / perhaps I would not be here /
perhaps the boys sleeping upstairs from me now
would not be here.

When you spend 8 minutes & 46 seconds / with your knee /
on another man's neck /
                      you block not just the passage
of air / into his body / but block air into all the possible
bodies / dependent on that man /
& his neck / to breathe / breathe / breathe /
breathe / breathe—

Citadel

This is not your body
it does not belong to you
it is not the one
that left the sallow rooms of home
circa 1980
never to return

this is not the body
who entered the hallway
of a college dormitory
and knew not a soul
who carried English books
like a soldier carries ammunition

this is not the body
that left the same college town
pregnant with a son
with a man you knew
would someday leave

this is not the body
who gave birth and
bid farewell to a womb
who carried two babies

this is not the body
who falls into anesthesia
and counts the stitches like shame

this is not the body
you return to
each murky dusk

this is the body you were told to smite
this is the body you hid inside
this is the body you cradled

this is the body
that knows the sound of a belt
removed before a beating

this is the body that knows
how to leave
like a song rising from nothing
like music leaving a cathedral

VIVIAN FAITH PRESCOTT

Tracking the Animal

There is this belly,
        it inflates and deflates with life,
filled with bubbling and gurgling

like water over stones,
like a low growl from the forest.

Me—this animal belly
        is a reindeer leaving tracks in snow,
with hoof prints stitched across tundra,

because years ago, a surgeon living
in a log cabin, left a line of sight,

a red-tacked trail
        from my belly button,
now a faint and well-traveled path.

My animal belly wiggles
and sways above hip,

stretches with cobra pose, and once
        jiggled to castanets.
This animal belly swells like bladderwrack

at menopause, a tent for memories. A belly
both satisfied and hungry

inspired, instinctive,
        has been shocked, scarred,
and scared, everything a belly can be—

mostly sacred—is even a wildland,
sticky with love.

ROBIN REAGLER

Contradictions in a Landscape of Human Love

In fairy tales sure a mother might feed
her daughter poison it happens sometimes it
happens to coincide with an illuminated
burden of a real diagnosis and upon repetition
It expands and fills up space say you're climbing
some hill thinking about *Paradise
Lost*—*the hell beyond, the hell
within*—and the earth swells into
a natural staircase and you scamper
up feeling your mojo kick in and think
how your daughter age 11 would struggle
to walk this trail and sure you find better
things to ponder allowing the mind
to wander until, back home, you have to give
the weekly chemo shot and all bets are off
She's not a princess you're not evil and yet

And yet here you go again the syringe
filled to the brim with thick yellow liquid
Carrie never cries but just asks, when will I
adjust to this and you think never you hope
never we must never accept the poison
we are given

SUSAN RICH

Post-Surgical Love Sonnet

For the first two weeks you live in awe
of the particles and atoms you meet—

the medullary rays of the oak dresser; the arc
of sandpipers in flight. Cotton sheets.

For fourteen days, you gaze into the garden—
astonished at the resilience of bindweed and horsetail.

You're an heiress of the inhabited world:
everything bagels and dinosaur kale.

Expeditions to the bathroom offer sentient thrills.
You urinate and defecate with ease—

And the bruised stars along your abdomen?
Zippers for survival. You're awake, alive, here still.

In the depths of the body there is a door, slightly ajar—
where you sense your temporal audacity, your power.

MICHAEL ROBINS

The Ordinary Inexplicable

On the first day in the warm, salty waters, & slipping beyond their break such fear came back to me from long ago & forever when, greedy for one last swim, we shuffled early through the sand & shallows, the pebble & shell before the depths & holy joy of floating, lifting with each wave midsentence &, before any sense or inkling of drifting a little farther out, the dark ocean pulled harder than whatever dig I could muster against its currents, just like that, & I forgot the conversation, what it was anyone might be saying for it felt like the nestlings tipped, like a hank of wet yarn unspooling or the weight of glass containing all the facts, measured recipes & what iota I might know of the 1860s, the end of loneliness & birds, the old summers climbing cherry trees with our brothers & sisters & not even time nor heart to think of my family sleeping somewhere right over there—maybe a stone thrown twice—tucked inside a rented house & yet I lived, long enough, to tell you how like music the panic filled my body, fell silent again & my friends, with whom I swam, never knew a thing.

ANNA V. Q. ROSS

All my poems used to end in sky

but now they end in sleep,
not sex, which, like looking at the sky
can be a way of moving farther and farther
away from yourself before you come
back down. But sleep is a going in
or back to what you aren't sure
you remember or ever want to see again.
When his older sister moved to her own room,
our son refused to sleep in his,
called it *the room where nightmares happen*.
This his first real loss, or the first he understood—
last year's burial of the cat out back
having mainly been an occasion for song
and shoveling—but this lack
of breath and sister scent drifting down
from the upper bunk, unbearable.
His whole life, he'd never had to go alone
into the dark, and why do we do this to ourselves,
when even lightning pairs its brief ecstatic fling
with thunder? *The very nature of materiality
is entanglement*, says the physicist, Karen Barad.
But I was talking about sex, which,
having been raised by Catholics,
I know full well is something one must do
but not discuss, and definitely not ask for,
even on the first hot day in June,
when your husband comes in from the garden

smelling like the tomatoes he's just planted
and sweat and dirt and whatever primitive
chemical you first scented years ago
in a dim cinderblock dorm room,
and both kids are out of the house
and there is the kitchen table bare
before you. *Don't do it!* my mother said
when I was twelve and she'd just walked in
from her job as a school nurse, having read
the second positive pregnancy test
from the second thirteen-year-old that week.
End of conversation.
Then, when I was twenty-eight, married, childless,
and in grad school, she gave me silk sheets
for Christmas. Just before she died, my granny
confided that grandad had been *a demon in the sheets!*
I hope that made up for twenty-two years
of pregnancies and sixteen births,
not all of them live.
Barad tells us *the other is not*
just in one's skin, but in one's bones.
And I know that even after birth, traces
of the child remain within the mother—
cellular echoes tinseled in the tissue.
So when our son was afraid to be alone,
we let him back into our parent bed nest,
where, cell by cell, he'd first learned how to sleep
inside of me. But each night, after he drifted
off, you carefully lifted him back
to his own room and then returned to me,
so we could not-speak together for a little while,
before we took our separate ways to sleep.

CHRISTOPHER SALERNO

Headfirst

Just a boy then, I was struck
        hard by a car and arced over

the roadside. Despite the pain I told
        no one. How the man driving

kept on driving. I hadn't yet found out
        about the body or velocity

or what a wound is, and how some bruises
        flower, spread like steam on the mirror

blurring all beauty. My mother
        says the '80s were terribly rapey.

She hisses into her rotary phone.
        Says a man may leave his voice

inside of a stranger forever, place something
        hard as a blood-flecked stone.

When I woke in the road, I rested
        my little chrome bicycle by the curb.

The smell of lilac, the sound of traffic
        starting up again in the street.

Shapes that keep us awake decades
        later. The fuck do I know about

all this thickness? Not the slant rhyme
        of fear & underwear. Haven't I

walked around with a killer's power,
        swaggering until now? But any boy's

teen years: days spent pursuant to puberty.
        The body as factory. I would

have driven high across this enormous
        darkness just to watch a woman

unbutton air. I should be writing this
        with fear, knowing I was danger.

HAYDEN SAUNIER

Performing Heart Surgery at 2 A.M. While Asleep

See, there's no blood.
The skin is a smooth waxy placket

that softly unbuttons.
Your breastbone splits neat

as a squeeze-open coin purse,
which is lucky because your terror of knives,

their cold shine
and quickness, their proof that time travels

in only one way
hasn't slammed shut the dream doors

allowing your hands to hold your chest wide
as you sit up in bed

and dump out the small frightened fist
that's your heart in your lap.

No surprise here.
You remember each scar, every mend, bite, and sizeable

chunk torn away or cut out,
shoveled back, re-attached, re-inflated,

but what makes you gasp
are the tools you've kept stashed, and their weight,

falling out of your chest—pocket knife, pliers,
a glue gun, two shrimp forks, electrical tape, black *and* yellow,

wire snips, needles and twine—just in case,
just in case, you need them again.

No wonder hearts hammer their hurts at the dark water margins
of sleep—it's the weight of repair

over years and this lightness
you feel once you lift your heart

back into place, seal your bones,
smooth your skin: that's the dream.

DIANE SEUSS

My hair? Oh, the color of a field mouse.

Its texture? Dust ball. My body, a world
of massive
disappointments. And I
quote: I didn't realize your stomach
would pooch over your two-piece.

Unquote.

Said at the beach when I was sixteen.
By my teacher.
That was the year dead
alewives washed up on shore in droves.
If they were coins, I would have been

rich, capable of liposuction and Miss

Michigan.
In this passion play, the body is Judas, fat
and misunderstood.
In the mirror,
its eyes are increasingly dead

fish. How did Jesus keep

his girlish figure?
Poverty, walking barefoot writing
parables in his head,

and getting flogged.
His was a starvation diet.

Bread, dates, olives.
A turtledove when he was lucky.

JACKIE SHERBOW

Razor Burn

My mother asks me about not shaving my legs,
so I learned: many things about my body
are a barrier to my pleasure.

On the ground, I am perceived. The hill behind the beach,
across from the ocean, is sand on asphalt. I feel tacky
fingers walk down the top of my vertebrae. We all need
oil to smooth things, to make things go.

I say yes when I am with you
so that I can say no at all other times.
I told you, I want to be all brain
or all body, but I'm always both.
We are a hologram until you unhurriedly
press your hand over my open mouth.

I say thank you. I am good.
I'm grateful for my objectness.

The beach road is dangerous to walk down,
especially when the whole family has a bad knee.
You pet my cheek before palming it, and I try
to be clean while looking out at the full ocean
through the window, and I fall asleep
with my arms in an X over my chest.

I hope I wake up
and am still here.

BETSY SHOLL

Thinking of Richard Avedon's Portrait of Isak Dinesen

Of course part of me wanted the tulips
   I just bought to stay in closed-up potential,
      and my own face to remain young,
untouched by grief and worry. But watching
   the slow-motion explosion each day,
      as they unfold, stems weakening, heads
bent, each petal's wilt and fall, I think of
   Isak Dinesen's face, how Avedon's camera
      emphasized crack and sag. Perverse,
she thought—his spotlight on her edge of decay,
   crushed and glorious. But perhaps he'd
      become sickened by all those models
slicked up for the glossies, and needed instead
   a sunken cheek, a face that had been through
      the press of heartache, gravity of time,
ruined enough to show a different beauty—
   a face that let itself be written on, as if
      that's how she came to write of others,
to imagine Babette after the Revolution
   fleeing Paris, that once high chef
      exiled to a dreary Norwegian town,
her cause lost, husband and son gone.
   Then the lottery ticket's sudden windfall
      she pours into one evening's brilliance
for townsfolk who can't seem to grasp
   what's been given. But for Babette—

      to be chef again, to practice her art
once more in that extravagant meal's wines
      and delicacies! Then in the aftermath,
          to stand among stacked dishes,
picked bones, bare stems and fallen petals,
     her eyes bright and fierce, having spared
        nothing, having spent it all.

DARA-LYN SHRAGER

Wednesday Bronchitis

With a throat full of swords and a milk-carton heart,
she walks a mile to the mall, crosses at the 4-way

light on Plymouth Turnpike, putting her whole hand
inside the broken metal mouth of a signal button

that once held the burn of summer and the bite
of frost in its wide "O". *Push*, she says to nobody,

then pilots her body, rotten with sick, over double
yellow lines. Four dollars will buy something nice.

NOEL SIKORSKI

In the car on the way to a family reunion

Inner suck
originating in the innermost room
of me dissipating me.
I am unbecoming
as my younger brother
and I speak
about putting our older brother
into a group home.
Newly displaced
from the room upstairs
where he's lived the last 35 years
to a room downstairs
in the basement,
our older brother
keeps wandering upstairs
to eat in the bathroom
next to his old bedroom,
which is where my nieces,
infants, now sleep, door locked
from the outside.
I have never been able
to protect my older brother.
Not when I was 5, or 6 or 8
and we lived in Korea,
or 13 or 17 when we were back
in the states. Not when
the other kids at school

would call him retard,
throw things at him and steal
his lunch money. Not
when the guard at our building
in Busan repeatedly molested him
in front of my eyes;
not when he was raped by
some man in Queens;
not when my mother screamed
she would put him in a home
if he didn't become someone else.

DREW SKELTON

Odonostalgia

Can I take a cast
of your teeth?
Nothing weird, I just
want to put them on my mantel.

I wish I'd started this hobby sooner.
I could have kept the smile of
my first-grade teacher
who didn't like me very much,
but whose jewelry, handed
out at her funeral,
I now wear.

There are casts I regret
taking.
I'm haunted by my ex's phantom
glint in my thigh's
retentive skin.

Some I never wanted at all—
my grandfather's chatter
atop the piano
whenever I sit to play. He bit
so deep into my mother
his imprints were mine
before birth.

I may resent yours one day.
I'm still learning trust,
and I think you'll be gone
sooner than I'd like, but then
you did smile
when I asked.

If I get dentures,
I hope they'll let me keep
my wonky incisor.
I like how it leans
against my tongue.

I like how my body
keeps itself
company.

MONICA SOK

The Hallway

I walked on ceilings when nobody was watching.
If I opened my stance, lowered my head, and pushed down my hands,
the ceiling became the floor. Nobody believed me.
They had not seen me do it. Nor had they paid attention
to my developing skills. The hallway was the best place to practice
my upside down world. To concentrate on walking,
I closed the brown shuttered doors to all the bedrooms.
Sometimes my hair would fly up, and I would have to tie it back.
When my head grew dizzy, I floated down on my back
and lay flat on the floor right below the light.
Who would believe in me if I did not believe in myself?
I knew the power I had could be tamed by the family.
To this day, nobody knows where I am when I am not home.

JOANNA SOLFRIAN

Mount Sinai

I have a paper calendar. I write my doctor appointments in this paper calendar with a pen. I have a lot of doctor appointments because I just had my Achilles reconstructed. (Technically, most are with a physical therapist, who is not a medical doctor but a child gymnast from Vermont. She flew home last weekend to see her fifteen year-old cockapoo.) Today I had a follow-up appointment at 9:45 a.m, with the surgeon. I hid my face in a mask and took the train to the Upper East Side and rode the elevator up nine floors with a woman in a wheelchair and a man with a cane. The man's eyes clicked down to my ankle. A red poppy bloomed through the gauze. When the elevator doors opened, I limped to the front desk and said my name. They had no record of me. They could not find me in the system. I have been here before, I said, many times. They asked for my license to prove I was a person. A young man typed my name. They still had no record of me. The surgeon is not even in the office, the young man said. Where is she? I asked, briefly wondering if she had stopped being a person as well. She is in her 59th Street office, they said. I did not know my surgeon was a person in two places. Your appointment is probably there, they said. But if I call here and make an appointment, I asked, how am I supposed to know it's there? That's a good question, they said. The young man handed me a business card with the 59th Street address. From my cell I called the number on the card. It rang at the desk I was standing at. By this time I was very late. I decided to go to the 59th Street address, so I called a cab before riding back down the nine floors to the lobby, where a different woman in a different wheelchair rounded a corner and ran over my foot. Out on the street, shocked by the light, I waited. I was shaking. As the cab pulled up, my phone rang. "You left your license up here," the young man said.

DONNA SPRUIJT-METZ

Dead Fathers Club

—after Psalm 38

I have poor
depth perception. I can't thread
a needle, can't get through.
You crossed over
long ago.
I raise my arms
to block the next
blow. And it will come.
I predict it with this
ruined machinery;
the punishment
for remembering is
another truth.
I am the patchwork woman,
my heart a low-
grade inflammation.
my skin a dated map, mottled
record of breakage,
no guide for this dark walk
towards God or blindness.
I eat my own hands
so as not
to touch another's.

HEATHER SWAN

Resurrection of the Body

After a long numbness
the slippery soul glides in,
and the tingling of return begins
like so many needles pricking
at once and everywhere,
the nerve endings exploding,
like roots sending tendrils
creeping beneath the surface,
wanting, and the air
interrogates my skin:
Where have you been?
Where were you hidden?
Did you think you could get away with that here?
The terrified pulse leaps
to the fingers that found it
and this body, all mouth, begins to move,
shift of out of stiffness, grasping and melting
in the April air, air of velvet, air of scent.
Hunger hungers. Oh God, I remember:
breath, breath of others,
sand and blood,
apples and salt,
oh yes, I remember now,
this torture,
this gift.

KELLY GRACE THOMAS

A Fertility Clinic is the Coldest Place on Earth

Before work / after work / you sit / business casual / and button-down
To your right / a bloodshot brunette / opens and closes Instagram
The blonde next to you / fades into the floor / Which of you is trying
hardest / not to cry / Who will break as you fill out form after form
When will you fail yourself / again / It's so easy for some / and others
$50K later / $100K later / You can't afford to be here / To want
Shiver at the sight / of test tubes / the icy grip of ultrasound jelly
Since fifth grade you've been warned / threatened / guaranteed / your
body would [   ] and when it came time [   ] / Back
then / in the cafeteria bleachers / you pulled your sweater over your
knees / as the projector flickered / and you learned / the danger / of
your [   ] / You don't want to be *that woman* / frostbitten / the
one who can't control / her fear / Who trades clipped voices with
doctors / as they say / *we wouldn't want you / to waste / your
money / your time our success rate* / Your small small window is
closing / So many small windows / pixels / a blizzard of gray / behind
eyes / behind glass / these seasons of maybe / where bellies grow
snowflakes where gender reveals flurry across the screen / And you're
sure / if you met these women somewhere else / a book club or Taco
Tuesday / you might even be friends / Instead you sit / together
Separate / Waiting rooms / for all your waiting / The nurse calls a
name / We all feel the chill / The blonde stands / No one makes eye
contact / Not even the nurse / *Back again?* / she asks / a knife
through winter

LYNNE THOMPSON

My Body Leaning Into

You might expect as centerpiece
West Indian Village With Figures

Dancing. Instead, my immigrant
parents buy a European imitation,

hang *Bal du Moulin de la Galette*
in our vestibule. All I can ask is

*are these the women you both pray
I will be?* It's impossible to tell where

each partner's shadow begins. Me? I
like Archibald Motley's *Saturday Night*

with its scarlet-clad heroine, her brown
arms unfolding from her body, her body

leaning into the rag & swing, one balding
man wishing he wasn't wishing, a shot of

bourbon & soda, bop & jive & jive & jive.
To stun Mother I say: *see the sommelier?*—

*how far he's willing to back-bend, cock-
tails listing to such risky angles just so*

*he can wallow in the woman's satisfaction
in simply being the center of everything?*

KC TROMMER

Agency

Give me a girl with a mouth and a story,
a live, ticking body and a heat for telling

Not the corpses men conflate with beauty
Not a dead girl whose story is always
someone else's is to tell

Give me a live girl, a mess,
one with a mouth for talking
One who doesn't know what she says
but knows it has to be said
One who knows exactly what she's saying,
if not what will ripple out of it

One whose mouth owns her,
eats her, spits her out clean

Give me a girl with a gift for burning,
one alight,
Who herself holds the match
Who doesn't want to die
Who wants life as much as fire wants oxygen
Who doesn't want someone else
to do the telling

Give me a real, live girl, better than neon,
better than pasties and siren song
better than calling all the boys to the yard

Give me a girl who wants for nothing,
because she turns and turns to herself
to find more, always

Give me a real girl   a live girl   a live wire   a firecracker
a ball buster   a fire starter   a hoot   a dame   a doll
a howl   a howler   a loudmouth   a potty mouth   a foul mouth
a bitch   a broad   a truth teller   a naysayer and ne'er do well
a churlish girl   a petulant twat
a cunt

Give me a girl, unscared, undead, whose mouth is alive
with her own story, who connects all the dots and comes screaming out
of whatever void they've hurled her into, comes screaming out
to blow it all open—

MICHAEL TYRELL

Intruder

Behind the blood-pressure bracelets
and their dangling black balloons, among
the gold circle coils of Trojans
waiting for consensus,
near the boxes of moon-dust gloves and sharps
but beyond the examining table's paper sheets
crinkling forward like newsprint etched with
the body's unreadables,
and close enough to the doctor who needs
the snake and silver spool to hear the inaudible heart—
the cricket caught somewhere inside, hidden.
More rasp than song. More song than siren.
Near the photograph
of the lungs like wilderness for sale
and the vent through which they say, make a fist,
this won't hurt a bit,
and the page on the waiting bench that begins
Of This Self-Planet
that Speaks Most Candidly in Earthquakes and Whispers,
I Will Always Feel Like an Intruder,
like a letter just started, a living will,
and the plasma silvering the funnels
to be tubed and set out all night
in the tin drugless bin
compact as a pet coffin, bright as a mailbox
from a century of letters.

LEAH UMANSKY

Reckoning

I tell myself, *forgive*. I need to forgive myself there,

                       and here.

I need a reckoning to reckon with the interior pine, shrub, windbreak,
    heartbreak, the mother-

                                   tongue of this life

                                                 of this body
                       the mother-

                                   tongue of mothering.

The mothering is a realization of grace   is a realization of the real and
    the unreal   and the reality that
nothing is truly either;
                 nothing
                       is more than the heart of the heart,
    and the heart of the interior of your body.

BARBARA UNGAR

AP Physics

> "One can never protect a single human being from any kind of suffering. That's what makes one so tremendously weary."
> —Mrs. Armfeld in *Smiles of a Summer Night*

Your son says, *Did you know
you exert a gravitational pull
on everything in the universe
and everything in the universe
exerts a gravitational pull
on you?* And that's what makes you
so tremendously weary,
you think, until you learn
there's no such thing
as gravity but rather space-
time curves like a stretchy
fabric and things roll towards
one another like balls that follow
grooved tracks around an incline

and then again that Einstein
was wrong: there is no time
or space at the tiniest
level, just quanta weaving
the net of what is, though
these are but crude metaphors

as you know from fasting,
eating peyote or giving birth
but which, to survive on the gross
scale of a body, you must forget.

And this, too, makes you
tremendously weary, or perhaps
it's just motherhood and age,
which also don't really exist.

LEE UPTON

Why Am I Not Invited to Your Party?

And what are your parties like without me?
Dancing? Is there dancing?
I used to dance. I danced like someone being stung
by ferocious bees. Agony was my means. I danced
to words I've never said aloud:
like *scullery* and *larder*.
And whenever what was playing stopped
I poured myself back into my body
like a deer at the side of a highway turning
away from the impulse to cross.
And exactly because I was all over the grid
someone left the party
saddled in the biggest gleaming body, hooved.
So if you keep me off your party list
I guess I can't make myself understand.
More than once I sacrificed my dignity
on the slab of a kitchen island.
More than once I danced off the cliff
and let everyone, first, jump from my back.
It was what we call wonderful, wasn't it?
It was. That's what it was.

SARA WALLACE

Thirty Years

You want to hold me
so we lie under the covers
in our underwear,
sticky stomachs touching,
your thumb worrying my elbow,
the commuter train rattling in the distance.
The smell of grease, turpentine and smoke
rises up from our neighbor's patio.
They're quiet, laughing just as loud
as the wind in the bushes,
so we'll need to be quiet too.
Our fifteen-year-old
will be gone only as long
as it takes to eat a slice
but we can't rush this—
after thirty years desire's rare,
shy as an albino fawn.
Soon you'll be dressed,
humming, stirring red spices
into a panful of grease and meat—
your body tired and slumped
but your feet dancing.
I'll stand at the sink
doing the few dishes,
my breasts hanging low
and forgotten
under my stained nightgown,

my nipples rough,
pocked as lemon peel.
Soon our son will walk
the unshaded strip of sidewalk
up the hill to our building,
knowing he should dawdle
but not really knowing why,
cars blowing up clouds of grit
as they pass him, a drift of song
that makes his face move
like a puddle's glossy meniscus
when the wind stirs it.
Our neighbors are eating now.
From above, the meat
on their glossy plates looks black,
the blood pooled like wet tar.
The cooling embers have turned grey,
a halo of smoke rising above the pit,
white ash sparking in the porch light.

JESSICA L. WALSH

It's Normal to Feel Your Body Has Betrayed You

Listen. As far as betrayals go, I started it, sucking
down Kool-Aid to Coke straight through until whiskey.
The Iowa years alone are worth a failed kidney, a fat liver. Miracle is
I made it this far before my body ran out of cheeks to turn.

O body, I begged you to take blow after blow, and you did, even
when I hated you, choked you with booze and gave you up to strangers,
threw punches with your hands, took punches with your nose,
even when I ate until I puked or ate because I planned to puke, when
I didn't eat or ate your weight—this very morning I chewed a cookie
then spat it into the disposal, like I could mock you and your hungry blood.

Body, if you choose today to begin your rough reckoning, if today
you pour all my secrets into charts and scans, if today is your cry
for mercy, I promise you what I feel is not betrayal but sad relief,
like a tired bully about to be felled. It's time, body, for you to tell on me.

PATRICIA J. WENTZEL

Miracle Weight Loss Drugs

I'm one of the lucky ones, if you can call it lucky to only have ultradian cycling Bipolar 1 disorder. My psych meds haven't declared war on my organs. They're mostly benign, caused a tremor in my right arm, gave me some trouble eating, writing, threading a needle, well okay, made that impossible along with taking pictures at the zoo. They were always blurry, a smear where a chimpanzee's face should be so you had to squint and wonder why anyone had bothered, as if the photographer had no standards which is what some people thought when they saw me roll into the room, enormously fat. I could feel them thinking it. *She has no self-discipline* or *She's let herself go* or *How could she let that happen?* which of course were all things I had thought about a fat person at one time or another when I was younger, thinner and less insane. I expect some strangers think that now when they see me limping along in my size 3X pants not realizing how much has changed since I recovered from decades convinced that I was evil like as in horror flick Evil and the only thing standing between me and my fiery end in an epic crash of my Toyota minivan into a hefty tree at freeway speeds was a bucket of KFC legs and thighs and the thought I would leave my children motherless, worse than that. They would be children who had been abandoned and left to wonder why their mother didn't love them and I knew they would think it was somehow their fault like I always thought I was to blame when mommy cried, that thought spinning through a brain with holes pre-drilled for delusion, the example of grandma nailing her front door shut with three inch spikes to keep the people who were cutting her hair in the night out of her house illustrating the existence of insanity in the family tree. A wiring diagram would have shown where to plug in trauma to evoke the maximum effect so that thought that I was to blame, maybe set me up for the delusional horror show theme and its convincing special effects. No way was I doing that to my kids who were also vulnerable to manifesting the surging tempest that was my insanity, an inheritance more dangerous than a teen on a Harley or a distracted skydiving instructor packing a chute, talk about insanity who would voluntarily jump out of a plane? Anyway, there was no way I was killing myself in this life, better to weigh 380 pounds which was also crazy thinking but made perfect sense the way it makes perfect sense for a grove of trees to feed the stump of a fallen comrade as if the surviving bit would thank them for keeping it alive in its debilitated state so it could sprout new trees that would one day tower over it, greedily shutting out the light. But maybe it would be grateful even then, grateful for even the half-life granted it as I was grateful for the bucket of KFC and the children who kept me alive and the meds and the tremor so I could one day say I had lost 140 pounds simply because I was no longer insane and when my doctor asked me how I did it I looked at her and all I could think to say was, *It was a miracle.*

ZOË RYDER WHITE

Eleven Impossibilities

When the lit front edge of the boat comes by
for the third or fourth time, I climb in,
lay my once-body down inside its once-body.
Rosy boat, curled and pale at the lip!
Not wood: petal. *Magnoliaceae*. Edible,
faintly spicy, built to convey a thought
from one end of hyperspace to the other.
An impossibility: hyperspace has "ends."
An impossibility: I fit in a petal boat.
An impossibility: I am currently unbodied.
An impossibility: I wear a blooming tree
around my shoulders for two weeks.
The dark is emptied
of its animals. There's nothing
to touch. The tree remains
undiminished. The stars
are fixed. Bosons take turns.
The door stays shut.

At the bottom of the boat, a porthole
opens in and out at the same time.
The universe-door is under that,
muscular, circular.
We fit through it; it fits through us.

REN WILDING

Snakeskin

I have a particular slither
in my chest coiling
me awake

my lungs will
not open

I sit against the bathroom wall
tiles slicked
with shower steam hissing
through me
a signal

as a child in the grocery store
with my mother
people stare

how could such a rattle come out
of that small throat
I'm trying to give myself
a warning

that my body
will be haunted
by what it sheds

MARIANNE WORTHINGTON

Low Ground of Sorrow

I'm not embarrassed when I see grown men cry
because my father cried. He cried big and out loud

his chin bobbing, his face melting into that low-
ground of sorrow he liked to sing about in his high-

lonesome voice. Sometimes he tried to explain
his crying mid-sob, how his voice would catch

and latch as water ran from his nose in honest
streams. Sobbing was a type of testimony,

evidence of faith in the grammar of sadness.
When his mother died he cried and gulped for air.

He sat up late in his chair and smoked Winston
after Winston until finally my mother called the doctor

who sent over pink liquid in a bottle which he refused,
the same way he pushed back food and sleep

for days. His tears mapped their crossing together,
for the mother who saved him after he suffered

a stroke at age 16, at school, carried home by
neighbors. He cried for his mother who shielded

him from his father who wanted him to get back
up, get back to work on the farm. He wept while

telling me how mean he treated his mother while re-
learning how to walk, how to speak. He was sorry

he had taken his injuries out on her, even
as he tried to make restitution the rest of his days,

caring for her in her very old age, tipping
the paperboy to lay the newspaper behind

the dry storm door, ferrying her to market,
to doctors, to the polls so she could vote,

checking on her daily until he found her one Saturday
morning still in bed, her teeth in the bedside glass,

and he cried, finally, without apology, broken down,
out in the open, a torrent of tears without ceasing while

the anniversary clock from his boyhood room ticked
its eulogy, its pendulum knobs twirling out a prayer.

JUSTIN WYMER

After, Still, I Want Someone to Want My Body

My sweat is dialogic: ancestral:
         which grayed figure
     never bathed or soothed
  and let the crow eat from his ear.
Which tore his children
        with a bullwhip. Which
ate pound cake with ramps
   as his daughter sucked
         a morphine patch.

I learned she bolted
      up from her pew at 16
         and swore to the congregation
   her breast was fixed
       to kill her, to keep
a pimply Bobby in her arms
        a child longer.

I was born blue. Who
     told the umbilicus to shoo
  from round the neck,
      that it was better I learn
  to breathe for *after*'s
    surely better
      than *before*.

Blue on an Oreo wrapper
     in the trash by a clear-

                    orange bottle
       meant she'd sold some peaches
                        and we'd have a roast,
                meant the day was good.

How many times
            did the pucker-faced angels
                handpainted armless
                        in the curio cabinet
        tell her the day was good,
                go on, peachy in a bed of needles
    with a spoon by the pillow.
                    She said she used it to feed
    the cherubs that spoke
            to her from the wallpaper.

Who found me in bed
        and pinched my grapes
        and promised   she'd make fruit
    salad when she got a break.
                Fruit cocktail can in the trash
            by travel-size Listerine
                means she'd been spotted
        after-hours
    at the tennis courts again,
                        kneeling.   Is this

            what you've wanted me
        to say
                    all along? Instead of
                "The crow cracked her egg
                        and fed the yolk
                    a pill
                the color of her hair?"

Acknowledgments

Jessica Abughattas. "Strip" from *Strip* (University of Arkansas). Copyright © 2020 by Jessica Abughattas. Reprinted by permission of the author.

Kim Addonizio. "Paris" forthcoming in *Exit Opera* (W.W. Norton, September 2024). Copyright © 2023. Printed by permission of the author.

Christopher Bakken. "Negative Theology." Copyright © 2021 by Christopher Bakken. First published in *Poetry Northwest*. Reprinted by permission of the author.

Ellen Bass. "Ode to Fat" from *Indigo*. Copyright © 2020 by Ellen Bass. Reprinted with the permission of The Permissions Company, LLC on behalf of Copper Canyon Press.

Jeffrey Bean. "Under my shirt, above my belt, there's an ache." Copyright © 2022 by Jeffrey Bean. First published in *Redactions*. Reprinted by permission of the author.

Jan Beatty. "Abortion with Gun Barrel" from *Jackknife: New and Selected Poems* (University of Pittsburgh Press). Copyright © 2017 by Jan Beatty. Reprinted by permission of the author.

Allison Blevins. "After Rembrandt's 'Self-Portrait,' Damaged by Acid in 1977." Copyright © 2022 by Allison Blevins. First published in

Split Lip Magazine. Subsequently published in *Handbook for the Newly Disabled: A Lyric Memoir* (BlazeVox, 2022). Reprinted by permission of the author.

Dustin Brookshire. "When I Was Straight." Copyright © 2023 by Dustin Brookshire. First published in *TAB: The Journal of Poetry & Poetics*. Reprinted by permission of the author.

Lauren Camp. "Woman's Body with Birds." Copyright © 2014 by Lauren Camp. First published in *Feminist Studies*. Reprinted by permission of the author.

Robert Carr. "Font" from *The Unbuttoned Eye* (3: A Taos Press). Copyright © 2019 by Robert Carr. Reprinted by permission of the author.

Eileen Cleary. "Flight of the White-Throated Sparrow" from *Child Ward of the Commonwealth* (Main Street). Copyright © 2019 by Eileen Cleary. Reprinted by permission of the author.

Nadia Colburn. "Outside the Sparrows Are Awake" from *I Say the Sky* (University Press of Kentucky). Copyright © 2024 by Nadia Colburn. Reprinted by permission of University Press of Kentucky.

Martha Collins. "Like Her Body the World" from *Casualty Reports* (University of Pittsburgh Press). Copyright © 2022 by Martha Collins. Reprinted by permission of the University of Pittsburgh Press.

Nicole Cooley. "My Mother's Nightgowns Smell Like Smoke." Copyright © 2022 by Nicole Cooley. First published in *SWWIM*. Reprinted by permission of the author.

Jessica Cuello. "Beauty." Copyright © 2023 by Jessica Cuello. First published in *Bennington Review*. Reprinted by permission of the author.

Ja'net Danielo. "For the Body as Poem." Copyright © 2023 by Ja'net Danielo. First published in *Diode*. Reprinted by permission of the author.

Julia Kolchinsky Dasbach. "Why write another poem about the moon?" Copyright © 2023 by Julia Kolchinsky Dasbach. First published in *Peste Magazine*. Reprinted by permission of the author.

Patrick Donnelly. "Prayer Over Dust" from *The Charge*. Copyright © 2003 by Patrick Donnelly. Reprinted with the permission of The Permissions Company, LLC on behalf of Copper Canyon Press.

Sean Thomas Dougherty. "Why Bother?" from *The Second O of Sorrow*. Copyright © 2018 by Sean Thomas Dougherty. Reprinted with the permission of The Permissions Company, LLC on behalf of BOA Editions Ltd.

Liza Katz Duncan. "Driving South, 10 Weeks Pregnant." Copyright © 2022 by Liza Katz Duncan. First published in *About Place*. Reprinted by permission of the author.

Iris Jamahl Dunkle. "Dear Body." Copyright © 2023 by Iris Jamahl Dunkle. First published in *NELLE*. Reprinted by permission of the author.

Kathy Fagan. "To My Hands on Their Birthday." Copyright © 2022 by Kathy Fagan. First published in *Couplet Poetry*. Reprinted by permission of the author.

Ann Fisher-Wirth. "'Tis a Consummation." Copyright © 2022 by Ann Fisher-Wirth. First published in *Thimble*. Reprinted by permission of the author.

Emily Franklin. "Plans." Copyright © 2021 by Emily Franklin. First published in *River Heron Review*. Reprinted by permission of the author.

Suzanne Frischkorn. "My Body as a Communist Country" from *Fixed Star* (Jackleg Press). Copyright © 2022 by Suzanne Frischkorn. Reprinted by permission of the author.

CMarie Fuhrman. "Dear Body." Copyright © 2019 by CMarie Fuhrman. First published in *Yellow Medicine Review*. Reprinted by permission of the author.

Jeannine Hall Gailey. "Self-Portrait as a Body Shaped by Illness" from *Flare, Corona*. Copyright © 2021 by Jeannine Hall Gailey. Reprinted with the permission of The Permissions Company, LLC on behalf of BOA Editions.

David Groff. "Days of 1986" from *Live in Suspense* (Trio House Press). Copyright © 2023 by David Groff. Reprinted by permission of Trio House Press.

Benjamin S. Grossberg. "My Mother Approves." Copyright © 2023 by Benjamin. S. Grossberg. First published in *Ploughshares*. Reprinted by permission of the author.

Jared Harél. "Achilles" from *Let Our Bodies Change the Subject* (University of Nebraska Press). Copyright © 2023 by Jared Harél. Reprinted by permission of the author.

Emily Hockaday. "The Heart Grows Full of Weeds." Copyright © 2023 by Emily Hockaday. First published in *Edda*. Reprinted by permission of the author.

Andrea Hollander. "The Wound" from *The Other Life* (Story Line Press). Copyright © 2001 by Andrea Hollander. Reprinted by permission of the author.

JP Howard. "in this house." Copyright © 2021 by JP Howard. First published in *Hyperallergic*. Reprinted by permission of the author.

Jessica Jacobs. "Sex, Suddenly, Everywhere" from *Take Me with You, Wherever You're Going* (Four Way Books). Copyright © 2019 by Jessica Jacobs. Reprinted with permission of The Permissions Company, LLC, on behalf of Four Way Books.

Patricia Spears Jones. "Dancer" from *The Beloved Community*. Copyright © 2023 by Patricia Spears Jones. Reprinted with the permission of The Permissions Company, LLC on behalf of Copper Canyon Press.

Meg Kearney. "Duckling, Swan" from *All Morning the Crows* (The Word Works). Copyright © 2021 by Meg Kearney. Reprinted by permission of the author.

Hyejung Kook. "Quick." Copyright © 2018 by Hyejung Kook. First published in *The Massachusetts Review*. Reprinted by permission of the author.

Michael Lally. "I Meant To" from *The Best American Poetry 2023* (Scribner). Eds. Elaine Equi and David Lehman. Copyright © 2023 by Michael Lally. Reprinted by permission of David Lehman.

Lance Larsen. "Quail Egg." Copyright © 2020 by Lance Larsen. First published in *Poetry*. Reprinted by permission of the author.

Eugenia Leigh, "Gold" from *Bianca*. Copyright © 2023 by Eugenia Leigh. Reprinted with the permission of The Permissions Company, LLC on behalf of Four Way Books.

Rebecca Lindenberg. "This Splendid Body." Copyright © 2023 by Rebecca Lindenberg. First published in Poem-a-Day / Academy of American Poets. Reprinted by permission of the author.

Mia Ayumi Malhotra. "On Memory" from *Notes from the Birth Year* (Bateau Press). Copyright © 2022 by Mia Ayumi Malhotra. Reprinted by permission of the author.

Cynthia Manick. "Dear Future Body" from *No Sweet Without Brine* (Amistad). Copyright © 2023 by Cynthia Manick. Reprinted by permission of the author.

Jennifer Martelli. "By August." Copyright © 2022 by Jennifer Martelli. First published in *Jet Fuel Review*. Reprinted by permission of the author.

Gail Martin. "Coming Back Body" from *Disappearing Queen* (Two Sylvias Press). Copyright © 2021 by Gail Martin. Reprinted by permission of the author.

Lynn McGee. "This Is It" from *Sober Cooking* (Spuyten Duyvil). Copyright © 2016 by Lynn McGee. Reprinted by permission of the author.

Erika Meitner. "Touch Cave." Copyright © 2022 by Erika Meitner. First published in the *Southern Indiana Review*. It was also featured on *The Slowdown* on March 16, 2022 and *Verse Daily* on March 29, 2022. Reprinted by permission of the author.

Jennifer Militello. "Odaxelagnia" from *The Pact*. Copyright © 2021 by Jennifer Militello. Reprinted with the permission of The Permissions Company, LLC, on behalf of Tupelo Press.

Fia Montaro. "Diastasis Recti Abdominis." Copyright © 2023 by Fia Montero. First published in *The Minnesota Review*. Reprinted by permission of the author.

Mary Morris. "Appointment with Dr. Siegel" from *Late Self-Portraits* (Wheelbarrow Books). Copyright © 2022 by Mary Morris. Reprinted by permission of the author.

Joshua Nguyen. "After I Was Mistaken for the Stripper While Delivering Barbeque to an All-White Bachelorette Party" from *Come Clean* (2021). Copyright © 2021 Joshua Nguyen. Reprinted by permission of the University of Wisconsin Press.

Lisa Olstein. "The Spell" from *Dream Apartment*. Copyright © 2023 by Lisa Olstein. Reprinted with the permission of The Permissions Company, LLC on behalf of Copper Canyon Press.

Iain Haley Pollock. "All the Possible Bodies." Copyright © 2023 by Iain Pollock. First published in *The Progressive*. Reprinted by permission of the author.

Connie Post. "Citadel" from *Between Twilight* (NYQ Books). Copyright © 2023 by Connie Post. Reprinted by permission of the author.

Michael Robins. "The Ordinary Inexplicable." Copyright © 2022 by Michael Robins. First published in *The American Poetry Review*. Reprinted by permission of the author.

Anna V. Q. Ross. "All my poems used to end in sky." Copyright © 2023 by Anna V. Q. Ross. First published in *The Arts Fuse*. Reprinted by permission of the author.

Christopher Salerno. "Headfirst" from *The Man Grave*. Copyright © 2020 by Christopher Salerno. Reprinted with permission of Persea Books, Inc.

Hayden Saunier. "Performing Heart Surgery at 2 A.M. While Asleep" from *How to Wear This Body* (Terrapin Books). Copyright © 2017 by Hayden Saunier. Reprinted by permission of Terrapin Books.

Betsy Sholl. "Thinking of Richard Avedon's Portrait of Isak Dinesen." Copyright © 2023 by Betsy Sholl. First published in *Maine Arts Journal*. Reprinted by permission of the author.

Monica Sok. "The Hallway." Copyright © 2023 by Monica Sok. First published in *The Washington Post*. Reprinted by permission of the author.

Donna Spruijt-Metz "Dead Fathers Club" from *General Release from the Beginning of the World*, Copyright © 2023 by Donna Spruijt-Metz. Reprinted with permission of Free Verse Editions, Parlor Press.

Heather Swan. "Resurrection of the Body" from *The Edge of Damage* (Parallel Press). Copyright © 2007 by Heather Swan. Reprinted by permission of the author.

Lynne Thompson. "My Body Leaning Into" from *Fretwork* (Marsh Hawk Press). Copyright © 2019 by Lynne Thompson. Reprinted by permission of the author.

Michael Tyrell. "Intruder" from *The Arsonist's Letters* (Backlash Press). Copyright © 2021 by Michael Tyrell. Reprinted by permission of the author.

Barbara Ungar. "AP Physics" from *After Naming the Animals* (The Word Works). Copyright © 2024 by Barbara Ungar. Reprinted by permission of the author.

Lee Upton. "Why Am I Not Invited to Your Party?" from *The Day Every Day Is* (Saturnalia). Copyright © 2023 by Lee Upton. Reprinted by permission of the author.

Zoë Ryder White. "Eleven Impossibilities" from *Hyperspace* (Factory Hollow Press). Copyright © 2021 by Zoë Ryder White. Reprinted by permission of the author.

Contributor Bios

Jessica Abughattas is the author of *Strip* (University of Arkansas), winner of the 2020 Etel Adnan Poetry Prize selected by Fady Joudah and Hayan Charara. Her short poetry film, *Dinner Party*, premiered at Mizna Twin Cities Arab Film Festival in 2021. Her poems appear in *Guernica, Los Angeles Review of Books, The Yale Review*, and elsewhere.

Kim Addonizio's latest poetry collection is *Now We're Getting Somewhere* (W.W. Norton, 2021). *Exit Opera* is forthcoming in September 2024. She is the author of seven other poetry collections, two novels, two story collections, and two books on writing poetry, *The Poet's Companion* (with Dorianne Laux, Norton) and *Ordinary Genius*, as well as a memoir, *Bukowski in a Sundress: Confessions from a Writing Life* (Penguin). Her awards include fellowships from the NEA and Guggenheim Foundation. *Tell Me* was a finalist for the National Book Award. She lives in Oakland, CA and teaches poetry workshops on Zoom. kimaddonizio.com

Kelli Russell Agodon is a bi/queer poet, editor, and educator from the Pacific Northwest. Her newest book *Dialogues with Rising Tides* (Copper Canyon Press) was a Finalist in the Washington State Book Awards and shortlisted for the Eric Hoffer Book Award Grand Prize in Poetry. She's the cofounder of Two Sylvias Press and teaches at Pacific Lutheran University's low-res MFA program, the Rainier Writing Workshop. She coedited *Demystifying the Manuscript: Essays and Interviews on Creating a Book of Poems* with Susan Rich and also co-hosts the poetry series, "Poems You Need" with Melissa Studdard. agodon.com / twosylviaspress.com

Lisa Andrews is the author of *The Inside Room* (Indolent Books, 2018) and *Dear Liz* (Indolent Books, 2016). Her poems have appeared in *Cagibi, Cordella, Gargoyle, Painted Bride Quarterly, POSTstranger*, and *Zone 3*. She received an M.A. in English literature and M.F.A. in creative writing (poetry) from New York University, where she taught in the Expository Writing Program, and worked with poetry students at Goldwater Hospital and Bayview Correctional Facility. She has had residencies at Blue Mountain Center, the Virginia Center for the Creative Arts, and the Vermont Studio Center. She lives in Brooklyn with her husband, artist Tony Geiger.

Subhaga Crystal Bacon (she/they) is a Queer poet living in rural northcentral Washington on unceded Methow land. She is the author of four collections of poetry including most recently *Transitory*, recipient of the Isabella Gardner Award for Poetry, 2023, from BOA Editions, and *Surrender of Water in Hidden Places*, winner of the Red Flag Poetry Chapbook Prize, 2023.

Christopher Bakken is the author of three books of poetry, most recently *Eternity & Oranges* (Pitt Poetry, 2016). He is also the author of the culinary memoir, *Honey, Olives, Octopus* (Univ. of California, 2013) and co-translator of the selected poems of the Greek poet, Titos Patrikios. Bakken serves as Director of Writing Workshops in Greece.

Mary Jo Bang is the author of nine books of poems—including *A Film in Which I Play Everyone, A Doll for Throwing*, and *Elegy*, which received the National Book Critics Circle Award. She has published translations of Dante's *Inferno*, illustrated by Henrik Drescher, *Purgatorio*, and *Colonies of Paradise: Poems* by Matthias Göritz. She's been the recipient of a Hodder Fellowship, a Guggenheim Fellowship, and a Berlin Prize Fellowship. She teaches at Washington University in St. Louis. Her translation of *Paradiso* is forthcoming.

Ellen Bass's poetry includes *Indigo, Like a Beggar, The Human Line*, and *Mules of Love*. Among her awards are Fellowships from the Guggenheim Foundation and NEA, The Lambda Literary Award, and four Pushcart Prizes. She co-edited the first major anthology of women's poetry, *No More Masks!* and she co-authored *The Courage to Heal: A Guide for Survivors of Child Sexual Abuse* and *Free Your Mind: The Book for Gay, Lesbian and Bisexual Youth*. A Chancellor Emerita of the Academy of American Poets, Bass founded poetry workshops at Salinas Valley State Prison and the Santa Cruz jails, and teaches in Pacific University's MFA program.

Jeffrey Bean (he/him) is the author of three chapbooks and the poetry collections *Woman Putting on Pearls* (2017) and *Diminished Fifth* (2009). His most recent chapbook, *Ella's Plan*, was chosen by Naomi Shihab Nye as the winner of the 2022 Poet's Corner/Maine Media Chapbook Contest. Recent poems appear or are forthcoming in *The Southern Review, Colorado Review*, Poets.org, *Sugar House Review, Poet Lore*, and *The Laurel Review*, among other journals. He is Professor of English at Central Michigan University, where he is a two-time winner of the Excellence in Teaching Award. jeffreybeanpoet.com

Jan Beatty's eighth book, *Dragstripping*, is forthcoming from the University of Pittsburgh Press, 2024. Her memoir, *American Bastard*, won the Red Hen Nonfiction Award. Recent books include *The Body Wars* and a chapbook, *Skydog* (Lefty Blondie Press, 2022). Other work includes *Jackknife: New and Selected Poems* (University of Pittsburgh, Paterson Prize) named by Sandra Cisneros on LitHub as her favorite book of 2019. Beatty worked as a waitress, abortion counselor, and in maximum security prisons. She is Professor Emerita at Carlow University, where she directed creative writing, the Madwomen in the Attic workshops, and the MFA program.

Allison Blevins (she/her) is a queer disabled writer. She is the winner of the 2023 Lexi Rudnitsky Editor's Choice Award from Persea Books and the 2022 Laux/Millar Poetry Prize from Raleigh Review.

She is the author of three collections, most recently *Cataloguing Pain* (YesYes Books, 2023). She is also the author of five chapbooks. Allison is the Founder and Director of Small Harbor Publishing. She lives in Minnesota with her spouse and three children. allisonblevins.com.

Marina Blitshteyn is the author of 2 poetry collections, *Two Hunters* (Argos Books, 2019), and *i take your voice* (Switchback Books, 2022), winner of The Gatewood Prize. Prior chapbooks include *Russian for Lovers* (Argos Books), *Nothing Personal* (Bone Bouquet Books), *$kill$* (dancing girl press), and *Sheet Music* (Sunnyoutside Press). She is working on a novel about motherhood and grief.

Dustin Brookshire (he/him) is the author of the chapbooks *Never Picked First For Playtime* (Harbor Editions, 2023), *Love Most Of You Too* (Harbor Editions, 2021), and *To The One Who Raped Me* (Sibling Rivalry Press, 2012). He's the co-editor of *Let Me Say This: A Dolly Parton Poetry Anthology* (Madville Publishing, 2023), which was named to the 2024 "Books All Georgians Should Read" list by the Georgia Center for the Book. Dustin is the curator of the Zoom-based Wild & Precious Life Series, founder/editor of *Limp Wrist*, curator of *Why I Write*, and director of virtual programs for Punch Bucket Lit. Find him online at dustinbrookshire.com.

Former Regional Director of the Poetry Society of America, final judge for the PEN's Best of the West award, the Kate & Kingsley Tufts Poetry Awards, and the international Laurel Prize, **Elena Karina Byrne** is a freelance editor, professor, and Programming Consultant & Poetry Stage Manager for The Los Angeles Times Festival of Books. Her five poetry collections include *If This Makes You Nervous* (Omnidawn Publishing, 2021). Elena's work can be found in *Best American Poetry, Pushcart Prize XXXIII, APR, POETRY, Paris Review, Poem-A-Day, Poetry Daily, Verse Daily*, and *BOMB*. Elena's writing screenplays while completing an essay collection entitled *Voyeur Hour*.

Lauren Camp serves as New Mexico Poet Laureate. She is the author of seven books, most recently *Worn Smooth between Devourings* (NYQ Books, 2023). Camp is a 2023 Academy of American Poets Laureate fellow, an emeritus Black Earth Institute fellow, 2022 Astronomer in Residence at Grand Canyon National Park, recipient of a Dorset Prize, and finalist for the Arab American Book Award. Her poems have been translated into Mandarin, Turkish, Spanish, French, and Arabic. laurencamp.com

Brenda Cárdenas has authored *Trace* (Red Hen Press), *Boomerang* (Bilingual Press), and three chapbooks. Her poems and essays have also appeared in anthologies and journals, including *Poetry*; *Latinx Poetics: The Art of Poetry*; *Grabbed: Poets and Writers on Sexual Assault, Empowerment, and Healing*; *Ghost Fishing: An Eco-Justice Anthology*; and *The Wind Shifts: New Latino Poetry*, among many others. She co-edited *Resist Much/Obey Little: Inaugural Poems to the Resistance* and *Between the Heart and the Land: Latina Poets in the Midwest*. She has served as Milwaukee's Poet Laureate and currently teaches Creative Writing and U.S. Latinx Literatures at University of Wisconsin-Milwaukee.

Robert Carr is a queer elder residing in central Maine with his husband. Their son, raised in a co-parenting relationship with a lesbian couple, is now thirty. Robert comes to poetry following a career in infectious disease response, where he administered programming for marginalized populations and the general public. He is the author of two full-length collections, published by 3: A Taos Press – *The Unbuttoned Eye* and *The Heavy of Human Clouds*. His poetry appears in many journals and magazines, including *The Greensboro Review*, *The Massachusetts Review*, and *Shenandoah*. Additional information can be found at robertcarr.org.

Eileen Cleary (she/her) is the author of *Wild Pack of the Living* (Nixes Mate, 2024), *2 a.m. with Keats* (Nixes Mate, 2021), and *Child Ward of the Commonwealth* (Main Street Rag Press, 2019), which received an honorable mention for the Sheila Margaret Motton Book Prize. She co-edited the anthology *Voices Amidst the Virus*, which was the featured text at the 2021 MSU Filmetry Festival. Cleary founded and edits the *Lily Poetry Review* and *Lily Poetry Review Books*, and curates the Lily Poetry Salon. A multi-pushcart nominee, her work is published widely in journals and anthologies.

Suzanne Cleary's books include *Crude Angel* and *Beauty Mark* (BkMk Press). Recipient of a Pushcart Prize, the John Ciardi Prize, and the Cecil Hemley Memorial Award of the PSA, her publication credits include PBSNewshour.org, *PoetryDaily*, *Best American Poetry*, *The Atlantic, Southern Review,* and *Poetry London*. Core Faculty in Converse University's MFA in Creative Writing Program, her website is www.suzanneclearypoet.com

Nadia Colburn is the author of the poetry books *I Say the Sky* and *The High Shelf*. Her poetry appears in *The New Yorker, American Poetry Review, Yale Review,* and elsewhere. She's the founder of Align Your Story Writing School, which brings together creative writing with mindfulness, embodied practices, and social and environmental engagement. See more at nadiacolburn.com, where she offers meditations and free resources for writers.

Martha Collins is the author of eleven books of poetry, most recently *Casualty Reports* (Pittsburgh, 2022) and *Because What Else Could I Do* (Pittsburgh, 2019); the latter won the Poetry Society of America's William Carlos Williams Award. Collins founded the UMass Boston creative writing program and taught at Oberlin College for ten years. Her website is marthacollinspoet.com

Nicole Cooley grew up in New Orleans and is the author of seven books of poems, including the forthcoming *Mother Water Ash* (LSU Press 2024), as well as *Girl after Girl after Girl* (LSU Press 2017) and *Of Marriage* (Alice James Books 2018). Her work has appeared most recently in *Poetry, DIODE,* and *Scoundrel Time*. She is a professor in the MFA Program in Creative Writing and Literary Translation at Queens College, City University of New York and lives outside of NYC with her family.

Jessica Cuello's most recent book is *Yours, Creature* (JackLeg Press, 2023). Her book *Liar,* selected by Dorianne Laux for The 2020 Barrow Street Book Prize, was honored with The Eugene Nassar Prize and The CNY Book Award. Cuello is also the author of *Hunt* (The Word Works, 2017) and *Pricking* (Tiger Bark Press, 2016). She is poetry editor at *Tahoma Literary Review* and teaches French in CNY.

Ja'net Danielo is the author of two chapbooks, most recently, *This Body I Have Tried to Write*, winner of the MAYDAY 2022 Poetry Micro Chapbook Editors' Choice Award. She is a recipient of a Courage to Write Grant from the de Groot Foundation, a Professional Artist Fellowship from the Arts Council for Long Beach, and the Telluride Institute's Fischer Prize. Her poems have appeared or are forthcoming in *swamp pink, Diode, Raleigh Review, Frontier Poetry*, and *In the Tempered Dark: Contemporary Poets Transcending Elegy* (Black Lawrence Press), among other places. Originally from Queens, NY, Ja'net lives in Long Beach, CA.

Julia Kolchinsky Dasbach is the author of three poetry collections: *40 WEEKS* (YesYes Books, 2023), *Don't Touch the Bones* (Lost Horse Press, 2020), and *The Many Names for Mother* (Kent State University Press, 2019). Her poems have appeared in *POETRY, Ploughshares, American Poetry Review*, and *AGNI*, among others. She holds an MFA from the University of Oregon and a Ph.D. in Comparative Literature and Literary Theory from the University of Pennsylvania. Recent awards include *Hunger Mountain*'s Ruth Stone Poetry Prize and *Michigan Quarterly Review*'s Prize in Nonfiction. Julia is Assistant Professor of English/Creative Writing at Denison University.

Patrick Donnelly is the author of five books of poetry, most recently *Little-Known Operas* (Four Way Books, 2019), and *Willow Hammer* (Four Way Books, 2025). He is director of the Poetry Seminar at The

Frost Place, Robert Frost's old homestead in Franconia, NH, now a center for poetry and the arts. Donnelly's translations of classical Japanese poetry with his husband Stephen D. Miller were awarded the Japan-U.S. Friendship Commission Prize for the Translation of Japanese Literature. Donnelly has lived with HIV for over 30 years.

Carol Dorf is a Zoeglossia and JSP fellow, whose books include *Theory-Headed Dragon,* and several chapbooks. Their work also appears in journals that include *About Place, Cutthroat, The Museum of Americana, Exposition Review, Unlikely Stories, Rise Up Review, Great Weather For Media, Slipstream, The Mom Egg, Sin Fronteras, The Journal of Humanistic Mathematics, Scientific American,* and *Maintenant.* They are founding poetry editor of *Talking Writing*, and taught math in Berkeley.

Sean Thomas Dougherty's most recent book is *Death Prefers the Minor Keys* from BOA Editions. He works as a medtech and caregiver in Erie, PA.

Liza Katz Duncan is the author of *Given* (Autumn House Press, 2023), which received the Autumn House Press Rising Writer Award and the Laurel Prize for Best International First Collection (UK). Her poems have appeared or are forthcoming in *AGNI, About Place, The Common, The Kenyon Review, Poem-a-Day, Poetry,* and elsewhere. She teaches English as a Second Language in New Jersey public schools.

Iris Jamahl Dunkle is an award-winning literary biographer, essayist, and poet. Her latest books include the biography *Charmian Kittredge London: Trailblazer, Author, Adventurer* (University of Oklahoma Press, 2020) and her fourth poetry collection *West : Fire : Archive* (The Center for Literary Publishing, 2021). Her next biography, *Riding Like the Wind: The Life of Sanora Babb,* is forthcoming from University of California Press in Fall 2024.

Kathy Fagan's sixth poetry collection, winner of the William Carlos

Williams Poetry Prize, is *Bad Hobby* (Milkweed Editions, 2022). *Sycamore* (Milkweed, 2017) was a finalist for the 2018 Kingsley Tufts Award. A 2023 Guggenheim Fellow, she teaches poetry at The Ohio State University, where she co-founded the MFA Program and co-edits *The Journal*/OSU Press Wheeler Poetry Prize Series.

Ann Fisher-Wirth's eighth book of poems is *Into the Chalice of Your Thoughts*, a poetry/photography collaboration with Willy Raussert (U Guadalajara Press, 2023). Her seventh is *Paradise Is Jagged* (Terrapin Books, 2023); her fifth, a poetry/photography collaboration with Maude Schuyler Clay, is *Mississippi*. With Laura-Gray Street, Ann is now coediting *The Ecopoetry Anthology: Volume II*, forthcoming 2025. A senior fellow of The Black Earth Institute, she received the 2023 Governor's Award for Excellence in Poetry from the Mississippi Arts Commission. Professor Emerita of English at the University of Mississippi, she also directed the program in Environmental Studies. She is married to Peter Wirth; they have five children and six grandchildren.

Emily Franklin is the author more than twenty books. Her work has appeared in the *New York Times*, *The Boston Globe*, *Guernica*, *JAMA*, *Threepenny Review*, *Cincinnati Review*, *The Kenyon Review*, and *Alaska Quarterly*, as well as read aloud on NPR and named notable by the Association of Jewish Libraries. Her debut poetry collection, *Tell Me How You Got Here*, was published in 2021. Her novel, *The Lioness of Boston*, based on the life of trailblazer Isabella Stewart Gardner, was published by Godine Books in 2023.

A grant writer by trade, **Karen Friedland**'s poems have been published in the *Lily Poetry Review*, *Nixes Mate Review*, *Constellations*, *One Art*, and others. She was nominated for a Pushcart Prize and had a poem hanging on the walls of Boston's City Hall. Her books are *Places That Are Gone* and *Tales from the Teacup Palace*. She lives in Boston with her husband and three critters. Karen lives with incurable, inoperable ovarian cancer, and is grateful for every moment she has left.

Suzanne Frischkorn's fourth book of poems, *Whipsaw*, is forthcoming in 2024 from Anhinga Press. Her most recent book, *Fixed Star*, (JackLeg Press) was a finalist for the 2022 Foreword INDIES Award. She is the recipient of The Writer's Center Emerging Writers Fellowship for her book, *Lit Windowpane*, the Aldrich Poetry Award for her chapbook, *Spring Tide*, selected by Mary Oliver, an Individual Artist Fellowship from the Connecticut Commission on Culture & Tourism, and a 2023 SWWIM Residency Award at The Betsy. She is an editor at *$ – Poetry Is Currency*, and serves on the Terrain.org editorial board.

CMarie Fuhrman is a mixed-race writer, teacher, and voice of the *Terra Firma* podcast. She believes in unique voices, the right to make decisions about one's own body, and the right to determine one's own identity. She has two dogs, Cisco and Apache, and lives unconventionally with her partner in a cabin in the woods of Idaho.

Jeannine Hall Gailey is a poet with MS who served as Poet Laureate of Redmond, Washington. She's the author of six books of poetry, including *Field Guide to the End of the World*, winner of the Moon City Press Book Prize and the SFPA's Elgin Award, and her latest, *Flare, Corona* from BOA Editions. Her work appeared in *The American Poetry Review*, *Salon*, *Ploughshares*, and *Poetry*. Her web site is webbish6.com. Twitter, Facebook, Threads and Instagram: @webbish6.

Sonia Greenfield (she/they) is the author of three full-length collections of poetry, including *All Possible Histories* (Riot in Your Throat, December 2022), as well as three chapbooks, including *Helen of Troy is High AF* (Harbor Editions, January 2023). Her work has appeared in the 2018 and 2010 *Best American Poetry*, *Southern Review*, *Willow Springs*, and elsewhere. She lives with her family in Minneapolis where she teaches at Normandale College, edits the *Rise Up Review*, and advocates for neurodiversity and the decentering of the cis/het white hegemony.

David Groff is the author of *Live in Suspense* (Trio House Press, 2023). His previous poetry books are *Clay* and *Theory of Devolution*. He is the coeditor of *Who's Yer Daddy?: Gay Writers Celebrate Their Mentors and Forerunners* and *Persistent Voices: Poetry by Writers Lost to AIDS*. An independent book editor, he teaches in the City College of New York MFA creative writing program.

Benjamin S. Grossberg's books of poetry include *My Husband Would* (University of Tampa Press, 2020), winner of the 2021 Connecticut Book Award, and *Sweet Core Orchard* (University of Tampa Press, 2009), winner of a Lambda Literary Award. He also wrote the novel, *The Spring Before Obergefell* (University of Nebraska Press, 2024), winner of the 2023 AWP Award Series James Alan McPherson Prize. He teaches at the University of Hartford.

Jared Harél (he/him) is the author, most recently, of *Let Our Bodies Change the Subject*, which was selected as the winner of the 2022 Raz/Shumaker Prairie Schooner Book Prize in Poetry (University of Nebraska Press, 2023). He's been awarded the Stanley Kunitz Memorial Prize from *American Poetry Review*, as well as the William Matthews Poetry Prize from *Asheville Poetry Review*. Jared lives with his wife and two children in Westchester, NY. For more info, visit: jaredharel.com

Dennis Hinrichsen is the author of eleven full-length collections of poetry, most recently *Dominion + Selected Poems* (Green Linden, 2024). Previous books have received the Akron, FIELD, Tampa, and Wishing Jewel Poetry Prizes. He lives in Michigan.

Camille Hernandez (she/they/siya) is a queer Black and Filipina author, educator, and facilitator. She considers herself a literary doula: tenderly providing readers with the strength to birth the unnamed vocabularies of our deepest ache to find pathways towards our collective liberation. Her debut book *The Hero and the Whore* debuted as Amazon.com's #1 new release in the Sociology of Abuse category. She lives in Anaheim, CA with her family.

Karen Hildebrand is the author of *Crossing Pleasure Avenue* (Indolent Books). She has been a human resource director, arts administrator, and magazine editor. She writes about dance for *Fjord Review* and *The Brooklyn Rail*, and can be heard on the *Jacobs Pillow Dance Festival* podcast. She holds an MFA from the Program for Writers at Warren Wilson College. Originally from Colorado, she lives in Brooklyn.

Emily Hockaday is the author of *In a Body* (Harbor Editions 2023) and *Naming the Ghost* (Cornerstone Press 2022), along with six chapbooks. She is a writer and editor out of Queens and can be found on the web at www.emilyhockaday.com. She was a 2022 Bethany Arts Fellow and a 2023 Queens Art Fund and DeGroot Foundation recipient. She writes about chronic illness, grief, ecology, parenthood, and the urban environment.

Andrea Hollander's sixth full-length poetry collection is *And Now, Nowhere But Here* (Terrapin Books, 2023). Her work has published widely, including a feature in *The New York Times Magazine*. Her many honors include two Pushcart Prizes (poetry and literary nonfiction) and two fellowships from the National Endowment for the Arts.

JP Howard is a poet, educator, and curator. Her debut poetry book, *Say/Mirror* (The Operating System, 2016), was a Lambda Literary finalist. She has received fellowships from Cave Canem, VONA, and Lambda Literary Foundation. She curates Women Writers in Bloom Poetry Salon.

Jessica Jacobs is the author of *unalone*, poems in conversation with Genesis (Four Way Books, March 2024); *Take Me with You, Wherever You're Going* (Four Way Books, 2019), one of Library Journal's Best Poetry Books of the Year and winner of the Devil's Kitchen and

Goldie Awards; and *Pelvis with Distance* (White Pine Press, 2015), winner of the New Mexico Book Award and a finalist for the Lambda Literary Award; and is the co-author of *Write It! 100 Poetry Prompts to Inspire* (Spruce Books/Penguin RandomHouse, 2020). Jessica is the founder and executive director of Yetzirah: A Hearth for Jewish Poetry.

Mara Jebsen is a performer of poems and professor of essay writing at New York University. A NYFA fellow in poetry, her work can be found in *Salamander, Sixth Finch, Jet Fuel Review, The American Poetry Review*, and *Painted Bride Quarterly*.

Melissa Fite Johnson is the author of three full-length collections, most recently *Midlife Abecedarian* (Riot in Your Throat, 2024). Her poems have appeared in *Ploughshares, Pleiades, HAD, Whale Road Review, SWWIM*, and elsewhere. Melissa is a high school English teacher and a poetry editor for *The Weight*, a journal for high school students. She and her husband live with their dogs in Lawrence, KS, where she co-hosts the Volta reading series at the Replay Lounge.

Arkansas-born **Patricia Spears Jones** has lived and worked in New York City since 1974. She is a poet, playwright, educator, cultural activist, and anthologist and has been appointed New York State Poet (2023-25). She is the recipient of 2017 Jackson Poetry Prize from *Poets & Writers*. She is author of *The Beloved Community* and *A Lucent Fire: New and Selected Poems* and 3 full-length collections and five chapbooks. At the Rauschenberg Residency, she published *Collapsing Forrest City, Photo Giclée*. Anthologized in *African American Poetry: 250 Years of Struggle and Song*; *Plume Poetry 8*; *2017 Pushcart Prize XLI: Best of Small Presses*; *WORD: An Anthology A Gathering of the Tribes*; *Of Poetry and Protest: From Emmett Till to Trayvon Martin*, and *Angles of Ascent: A Norton Anthology of Contemporary African-American Poets*, and in journals such as *About Place Journal; Paterson Literary Review; Cutthroat Journal*; alinejournal.com/convergence; *The New Yorker*, and *The Brooklyn Rail*.

Jen Karetnick is the author of five full-length poetry collections, the most recent of which is *Inheritance with a High Error Rate* (January 2024), winner of the 2022 Cider Press Review Book Award. She is also the author of six poetry chapbooks, including *What Forges Us Steel: The Judge Judy Poems* (Alternating Current Press, 2024) and *The Crossing Over* (March 2019), winner of the 2018 Split Rock Review Chapbook Competition. Co-founder/managing editor of *SWWIM Every Day*, she has been supported by Vermont Studio Center, Wildacres Retreat, Mother's Milk, and elsewhere. Based in Miami, she lives with multiple chronic illnesses.

Meg Kearney's *All Morning the Crows*, winner of the Washington Prize for poetry, was published by The Word Works in 2021. Meg is also author of *An Unkindness of Ravens* and *Home By Now*, winner of the PEN New England L.L. Winship Award; a heroic crown/chapbook, *The Ice Storm* (in its 3rd printing); and three verse novels for teens. Her award-winning picture book, *Trouper*, is illustrated by E.B. Lewis. Meg's poetry has been featured on Garrison Keillor's *A Writer's Almanac* and Ted Kooser's *American Life in Poetry*. She lives in New Hampshire and directs the Solstice MFA in Creative Writing Program at Lasell University. megkearney.com.

Hyejung Kook's poetry has appeared or is forthcoming in *POETRY, Denver Quarterly, Poetry Northwest, Verse Daily, The Massachusetts Review, Pleiades, Hyphen Magazine,* and elsewhere. Other works include essays in *The Critical Flame* and *Poetry as Spellcasting* (North Atlantic Books, 2023) and a chamber opera libretto. Her poems have been anthologized and also set to art song. Born in Seoul, Hyejung now lives in Kansas with her husband and their two children. She is a Fulbright grantee and Kundiman fellow.

Michael Lally's poetry honors include the NYC 92nd St. Y Poetry Center's 1972 Discovery Award for *The South Orange Sonnets*; two National Endowment for the Arts Poetry Fellowships; 1997 PEN Oakland Award for *Cant Be Wrong*; 2000 American Book Award for

It's Not Nostalgia. In 2018, *Another Way to Play: Poems 1960-2017* came out. His most recent book is *Say It Again: An Autobiography in Sonnets* (Beltway Editions, 2024). Also known as an actor for his work in TV and movies. Writes the blog *Lally's Alley* on poetry, politics, movies, and other arts. "I Meant To" reflects Lally's living with Parkinson's Disease.

Lance Larsen has published six poetry collections, most recently *Making a Kingdom of It* (Univ. of Tampa Press, 2024). His awards include a Pushcart Prize, the Tampa Review Prize, and fellowships from Ragdale, Sewanee, the Anderson Center, and the NEA. In 2017 he completed a five-year appointment as Utah's Poet Laureate. He teaches at BYU.

Viola Lee graduated from NYU with an MFA in Poetry. Her book *Lightening after the Echo* was published by Another New Calligraphy. She has published poems in literary journals throughout the US, and has published in *Barrow Street*, *Bellevue Literary Review*, and *Another Chicago Magazine*. Her poems recently won finalist in the *Pleiades* Prufer Poetry Prize and the 2022 *Mississippi Review* Poetry Prize. Her manuscript *The Only Home* was a finalist in the 2023 Switchback Books' Gatewood Prize and was also a Semi-finalist in the 2023 Perugia Press Poetry Prize. She lives in Chicago with her husband, son and daughter. She teaches 4th, 5th and 6th graders.

Eugenia Leigh is a Korean American poet and the author of *Bianca* (Four Way Books, 2023) and *Blood, Sparrows and Sparrows* (Four Way Books, 2014). Her poems and essays have appeared in publications such as *TIME*, *The Atlantic*, *The Nation*, *Poetry*, *Ploughshares*, *Waxwing*, and the *Best of the Net* anthology. The recipient of Poetry magazine's Bess Hokin Prize as well as awards and fellowships from *Poets & Writers*, Kundiman, and elsewhere, Eugenia received her MFA from Sarah Lawrence College and serves as a Poetry Editor at *The Adroit Journal* and as the Valentines Editor at *Honey Literary*.

Rebecca Lindenberg is the author of *Our Splendid Failure to Do the Impossible* (BOA Editions, 2024), *The Logan Notebooks* (Mountain West Poetry Series, 2014), winner of the 2015 Utah Book Award, and *Love, an Index* (McSweeneys, 2012). She's an Associate Professor at the University of Cincinnati, where she also serves as Poetry Editor of the *Cincinnati Review*.

Matthew Lippman is the author of six poetry collections. His latest book *Mesmerizingly Sadly Beautiful* (2020) is published by Four Way Books. It was the recipient of the 2018 Levis Prize. His next collection, *We Are All Sleeping With Our Sneakers On*, is published by Four Way Books in 2024.

Margaree Little (she/they) is the author of *REST* (Four Way Books, 2018), winner of the 2018 Balcones Poetry Prize and the 2019 Audre Lorde Award for Lesbian Poetry. Her poems, criticism, and translations appear widely, including in *American Poetry Review, New England Review, Kenyon Review Online, Asymptote*, and *The Brooklyn Rail (In Translation)*. She is the recipient of awards, fellowships, and residencies from the Rona Jaffe Foundation, *The Kenyon Review*, Bread Loaf, the Camargo Foundation, and the Arizona Commission on the Arts, among others. She lives in Tucson and teaches at the University of Arizona.

Mia Ayumi Malhotra is the author of *Mothersalt* (Alice James Books, 2025) and *Isako Isako*, a California Book Award finalist and winner of the Alice James Award, Nautilus Gold Award, and Maine Literary Award. She is also author of the chapbook *Notes from the Birth Year*, winner of the Bateau Press BOOM Contest. She lives in Northern California with her family.

Christine Malvasi earned her M.F.A. in Creative Writing from New York University, where she teaches as a clinical associate professor. She's the editor of *Challenges for the Delusional*, an anthology of writing exercises and the poems that they inspired. As a writer and performer, she's participated in residencies and fellowships throughout the United States and Italy.

Cynthia Manick is the author of *No Sweet Without Brine* (Amistad-HarperCollins, 2023), which received 5 stars from Roxane Gay and was selected as a New York Public Library Best Book of 2023; editor of *The Future of Black: Afrofuturism, Black Comics, and Superhero Poetry*; winner of the Lascaux Prize in Collected Poetry; and author of *Blue Hallelujahs*. She has received fellowships from Cave Canem, Hedgebrook, and MacDowell among other foundations. Manick's work has appeared in the Academy of American Poets *Poem-A-Day Series, Brooklyn Rail, The Rumpus,* and other outlets. She lives in New York but travels widely for poetry.

Fred Marchant is the author of five books of poetry, the most recent of which is *Said Not Said* (Graywolf Press, 2017). He is the editor of *Another World Instead*, a selection of the early poems of William Stafford. He is also co-editor (with Jennifer Barber and Jessica Greenbaum) of *Tree Lines*, a collection of contemporary American poems related to the trees and forests in our lives. Marchant is an emeritus professor of English and founding director of the Poetry Center at Suffolk University in Boston.

Jennifer Martelli (she/her) is the author of *The Queen of Queens*, winner of the Italian American Studies Association Book Award and named a "Must Read" by the Massachusetts Center for the Book and *My Tarantella*, also a "Must Read," and finalist for the Housatonic Book Award. Her work has appeared in *Poetry*, The Academy of American Poets *Poem-a-Day, The Tahoma Literary Review, Folio, Jet Fuel Review, The Northwest Review, Tab: A Journal of Poetry,* and elsewhere. Jennifer Martelli has twice received grants for poetry from the Massachusetts Cultural Council and is co-poetry editor of *MER*. jennmartelli.com

Gail Martin's third collection, *Disappearing Queen*, won the Two Sylvias Press Wilder prize in 2021. *Begin Empty-Handed* won the Perugia Press Poetry prize in 2013 and won the Housatonic Book Award for Poetry. *The Hourglass Heart* (New Issues) was published in 2003. Martin works as a psychotherapist in Kalamazoo, Michigan.

A native of Liberia who was raised in Philadelphia, **Trapeta B. Mayson** was the 2020-2021 Philadelphia Poet Laureate and is the founder of Healing Verse Philly and the Healing Verse Poetry Line, 1-855-PoemRx2. In 2021, she was named an Academy of American Poets Laureate Fellow. Mayson is also a Cave Canem and Pew Fellow. She earned her BA in Political Science and Master's Degrees in Social Services and Business from Bryn Mawr Graduate School of Social Work and Social Research and Villanova University School of Business. Mayson is a published author, teaching artist, and curator of numerous artistic and civic projects. She is a licensed clinical social worker, community arts practitioner, and administrator at a community mental health agency. She resides in Philadelphia.

Caitlin Grace McDonnell is a queer/bi single-mother, highly sensitive poet, writer, feminist, yogi, cold-water plunger, and longtime adjunct writing instructor. She's published poems and essays, two books: *Pandemic City* and *Looking for Small Animals*, and a chaplet, *Dreaming the Tree*. She resides in Brooklyn with her teenage daughter and weird dog Olive, but also escapes to a lake upstate. She is 54, has seen the void, and is not done becoming.

Lynn McGee is the author of the poetry collections *Tracks* (Broadstone Books, 2019), *Sober Cooking* (Spuyten Duyvil, 2016), and two award-winning poetry chapbooks: *Heirloom Bulldog* (Bright Hill Press) and *Bonanza* (Slapering Hol Press). Lynn McGee and José Pelauz are co-authors of the children's book *Starting Over in Sunset Park* (Tilbury House Publishers, 2021). Lynn's forthcoming poetry collection from Broadstone Books, *Science Says Yes*, looks at a planet reeling with unnatural disasters and the cackle of technology, a panoramic view offset by the pursuit of happiness and gratitude. lynnmcgee.com

Erika Meitner is the author of six books of poems, including *Holy Moly Carry Me* (BOA Editions, 2018), winner of the National Jewish Book Award and a finalist for the National Book Critics Circle Award in poetry; and *Useful Junk* (BOA Editions, 2022). Meitner is currently a professor of English at the University of Wisconsin-Madison.

Jennifer Militello is the author of *The Pact* (Tupelo Press/Shearsman Books, 2021) and the memoir *Knock Wood*, winner of the Dzanc Nonfiction Prize (Dzanc Books, 2019), as well as four previous collections of poetry. Her work has appeared in *Best American Poetry*, *American Poetry Review*, *The Nation*, *The New Republic*, *The Paris Review*, and *Tin House*. She teaches in the MFA program at New England College.

Sam Moe (she/they) has received residencies from VCCA and Château d'Orquevaux. She is the recipient of a 2023 St. Joe Community Foundation Poetry Fellowship from Longleaf Writers Conference. Her work has appeared or is forthcoming from *Peatsmoke Journal*, *The Indianapolis Review*, *Sundog Lit*, and others. Her first full-length collection, *Heart Weeds*, was published with Alien Buddha Press (Sept. '22) and her second full-length collection *Grief Birds* was published with Bullshit Lit (Apr. '23). Her third full-length *Cicatrizing the Daughters* is forthcoming from FlowerSong Press.

Fia Montero holds a BFA in Art and Design from Iowa State University, and a BSHS in Pre-Medical Science from Mercy College of Health Sciences. Her work has appeared in *West Trestle Review*, *Passengers Journal*, *Minnesota Review*, and elsewhere. She lives in Iowa.

Caridad Moro-Gronlier is the author of *Tortillera* (TRP 2021), winner of The TRP Southern Poetry Breakthrough Series: Florida, The 2022 Eric Hoffer Book Award Honorable Mention, 2022 First

Horizon Award Finalist and 2022 International Latino Book Award Honorable Mention, as well as the chapbook *Visionware* (Finishing Line Press 2009). She is a Contributing Editor for *Grabbed: Poets and Writers Respond to Sexual Assault* (Beacon Press, 2020) and Associate Editor for *SWWIM Every Day,* an online daily poetry journal for women identifying poets. She resides in Miami, Florida, with her wife and son.

Mary Morris is the author of three books of poetry: *Enter Water, Swimmer* (runner-up for the X.J. Kennedy Prize), *Dear October* (Arizona-New Mexico Book Award), and *Late Self-Portraits* (selected by Leila Chatti for the MSU Wheelbarrow Book Prize). Morris received the Rita Dove Award and has been invited to read her poems at the Library of Congress, which aired on NPR. Her poems are published in *Poetry, Poetry Daily, Verse Daily, Prairie Schooner,* and *North American Review.* Kwame Dawes selected her work for *American Life in Poetry* from the Poetry Foundation. water400.org

Alicia Rebecca Myers' poems and essays have appeared in *Best New Poets* (2015, 2021, 2023), *Creative Nonfiction, FIELD, Gulf Coast, SWWIM, december, Threadcount,* and *The Rumpus.* Her first full-length manuscript *Warble* was a finalist for the 2023 Akron Poetry Prize, and her chapbook of poems, *My Seaborgium* (Brain Mill Press), was winner of the inaugural Mineral Point Chapbook Series. She lives with her husband, son, and pitchow Gumbo in upstate NY.

Poet, essayist, translator, and Fulbright Scholar, **Rachel Neve-Midbar**'s collection *Salaam of Birds* (Tebot Bach 2020) was chosen by Dorothy Barresi for the Patricia Bibby First Book Prize. She is also the author of the chapbook *What the Light Reveals* (Tebot Bach, 2014, winner of The Clockwork Prize). She is currently a Fulbright postdoc in Israel translating the poems of Holocaust poet Abba Kovner. Rachel is also the co-editor of *Stained: an anthology of writing about menstruation* (Querencia Press, July 2023).

Joshua Nguyen is the author of *Come Clean* (University of Wisconsin Press, 2021), winner of the Felix Pollak Prize in Poetry, the Writers' League of Texas Discovery Award, and the Mississippi Institute of Arts & Letters Poetry Award. He is also the author of the chapbooks, *American Lục Bát for My Mother* (Bull City Press, 2021) and *Hidden Labor & The Naked Body* (Sundress Publications, 2023). He is a Vietnamese-American writer, a collegiate national poetry slam champion (CUPSI), and a native Houstonian. He received his MFA/PhD from The University of Mississippi. He currently teaches at Tufts University.

Rebecca Hart Olander's poetry and collaborative visual and written work has appeared in print, online, and in multiple anthologies. Her books include *Dressing the Wounds* (dancing girl press, 2019) and *Uncertain Acrobats* (CavanKerry Press, 2021), a finalist for the Massachusetts Book Award. Rebecca has taught at Amherst and Smith colleges and Westfield State University and works with poets in the Maslow Family Graduate Program. She's the editor/director of Perugia Press.

Lisa Olstein is the author of five poetry collections, most recently *Dream Apartment* (Copper Canyon Press). Her nonfiction includes *Pain Studies* (Bellevue Literary Press), a book-length lyric essay, and *Climate* (Essay Press), an exchange of epistolary essays with the poet Julie Carr.

Alixen Pham is a Best New Poets 2022 finalist and Best of the Net-nominated multidisciplinary artist/poet/writer with numerous publications including *The Slowdown* featuring Ada Limon, *Salamander, Tahoma Literary Review, Rust+Moth*, and *Apogee Journal*. Since 2022, she curates adult authors of poetry, fiction and nonfiction works for the Festival of Asian American and Pacific Islander Books in Long Beach, CA. Alixen facilitates weekly generative poetry workshops through The Poetry Salon. She is the recipient of the City of West Hollywood 2022 Artist Grant, Brooklyn Poets Fellowship & Scholarships, AWP Mentee Program, PEN Center Fiction Scholarship and others. Her website: alixenpham.com

Maya Pindyck is the author of three books of poetry, most recently *Impossible Belonging* (Anhinga Press, 2023), winner of the Philip Levine Prize for Poetry and a finalist for the National Jewish Book Award. She is co-author of *A Poetry Pedagogy for Teachers* (Bloomsbury, 2022). Her honors include a National Endowment for the Arts Fellowship and a Poetry Society of America Chapbook Fellowship. She lives in Philadelphia where she is an assistant professor and director of Writing at Moore College of Art & Design.

Iain Haley Pollock is the author of three poetry collections, *Spit Back a Boy, Ghost, Like a Place,* and *All the Possible Bodies,* forthcoming from Alice James Books in September 2025. Pollock has received several honors for his work including the Cave Canem Poetry Prize, the Alice Fay di Castagnola Award from the Poetry Society of America, a 2023 NYSCA/NYFA Artist Fellowship in Poetry, the Bim Ramke Prize for Poetry from *Denver Quarterly* and a nomination for an NAACP Image Award. He serves as Director of the MFA Program in Creative Writing at Manhattanville College in Purchase, NY.

Connie Post served as the first Poet Laureate of Livermore, California. Her work has appeared in *Calyx, Comstock Review, River Styx, The American Journal of Poetry, Spoon River Poetry Review,* and *Verse Daily*. Her Awards include the Crab Creek Review Award, Liakoura award, and the Caesura award. She has three full length collections and three chapbooks. Her two 2023 collections include *Between Twilight* by New York Quarterly books and *Broken Metronome* (Glass Lyre Press). *Between Twilight* was a finalist for the Best Book Awards and *Broken Metronome* was named the winner for a poetry chapbook in the American Fiction Awards.

Vivian Faith Prescott (she/her) is a bi+ writer, born and raised on a small island, Wrangell, Kaachxana.áak'w, in Southeast Alaska. She lives and writes as a climate witness in Lingít Aaní at her family's fishcamp on the land of the Shtax'héen Kwáan. She is a member of the Pacific Sámi Searvi and a founding member of Community Roots, the first LGBTQIA+ group on the island.

Robin Reagler is a poet and parent who lives in Houston, Texas. Her most recent books are *Night Is This Anyway* (Lily Poetry, 2022) and *Into The The* (Backlash Books, 2021).

Susan Rich is a Jewish-Ukrainian poet, author of six poetry books including *Blue Atlas* from Red Hen Press. Recent work appears in the *Harvard Review, Poetry Ireland,* and The Academy of American Poets *Poem-a-Day*. Her poetry has earned awards from PEN USA and the Fulbright Foundation. Co-editor of *Demystifying the Manuscript: Creating a Book of Poems*, Susan teaches at Highline College and lives in Seattle. She directs Poets on the Coast: A Writing Retreat for Women. Visit her online at susanrich.com

Michael Robins is the author of five collections of poetry, including *The Bright Invisible* (Saturnalia Books, 2022) and *People You May Know* (Saturnalia Books, 2020). He lives in Lake Charles, Louisiana, where he teaches creative writing in the MFA program at McNeese State University and edits *The McNeese Review*.

Anna V. Q. Ross's most recent book, *Flutter, Kick*, won the Benjamin Saltman Poetry Award from Red Hen Press, the Julia Ward Howe Award in Poetry from the Boston Authors Club, and was named a Best New Poetry Book by the New York Public Library. Her work appears in *The Kenyon Review, Harvard Review, The Missouri Review, The Nation*, and elsewhere. A poetry editor for *Salamander*, Anna teaches at Tufts University and through the Emerson Prison Initiative. She lives with her family in Dorchester, MA, where she raises chickens. Find her at annavqross.com.

Christopher Salerno is the author of five books of poetry. His latest book, *The Man Grave*, won the Lexi Rudnitsky Editor's Choice Award from Persea Books. Previous books include *Sun & Urn* (UGA Poetry Prize), *ATM* (Georgetown Poetry Prize), *Minimum Heroic* (Mississippi Review Poetry Prize), and *Whirligig*. His poetry has received the Glenna Luschei Award from *Prairie Schooner*, The Founders Prize from *RHINO Magazine*, the Two Sylvias Press Chapbook Award, the *Laurel Review* Chapbook Prize, and a New Jersey State Council on the Arts fellowship. He teaches Creative Writing at William Paterson University in New Jersey where he serves as Director of Writing Across the Curriculum.

Hayden Saunier is the author of *A Cartography of Home* and four other collections of poetry. Her work has been awarded a Pushcart Prize, the *Rattle* Poetry Prize, the Pablo Neruda Prize, published widely in journals such as *32 Poems, diode, Pedestal, Plume, VQR*, and featured on *Poetry Daily, Verse Daily*, and *The Writers Almanac*. Hayden is the founder and director of No River Twice, an interactive, audience-driven, poetry performance group.

Diane Seuss is the author of six books of poetry, including *Modern Poetry* (Graywolf Press 2024) and *frank: sonnets* (Graywolf Press 2021), the winner of the PEN/Voelcker Prize, the *Los Angeles Times* Book Prize, the National Book Critics Circle Award, and the Pulitzer Prize. Seuss was a 2020 Guggenheim Fellow. She was raised by a single mother in rural Michigan, which she continues to call home.

Jackie Sherbow is the Queens, NY author of *Harbinger* (Finishing Line Press, 2019), the publisher at THRASH Press, and the senior managing editor of *Ellery Queen's Mystery Magazine* and *Alfred Hitchcock's Mystery Magazine*. Their poems have appeared in places like *Sierra Nevada Review* and *Luna Luna*, their fiction in *Mystery Magazine*, and their poems and short stories have been anthologized.

Betsy Sholl's tenth collection of poetry is *As If a Song Could Save You* (University of Wisconsin Press, 2022), winner of the Four Lakes Prize. Her ninth collection is *House of Sparrows: New and Selected Poems* (University of Wisconsin, 2019). She teaches in the MFA in Writing Program of Vermont College of Fine Arts and served as Poet Laureate of Maine from 2006 to 2011. She was awarded the 2020 Distinguished Achievement Award from Maine Writers and Publishers Alliance.

Dara-Lyn Shrager is the co-founder and co-editor of *Radar Poetry*. She lives in Princeton, NJ with her family, including two small dogs. Her poetry collection, *Whiskey, X-Ray, Yankee*, was published by Barrow Street Books in 2018. Her poems appear or are forthcoming in many journals, including *The Iowa Review, The Los Angeles Review, Crab Creek Review, Southern Humanities Review, Barn Owl Review, Pacifica Literary Review* and *Nashville Review*. Learn more at: daralynshrager.com and radarpoetry.com

Noel Sikorski. Her work has been published in *The American Poet; Painted Bride Quarterly; The Georgetown Review; The Bellevue Literary Review; Action, Spectacle;* and *The Delmarva Review*.

Drew Skelton (he/they) was born in Tennessee where they attended Nashville School of the Arts. He graduated from Hendrix College in 2024 with a Bachelor's in Creative Writing. He was nominated for the Southern Literary Festival, and he won first place in the Aonian fiction writing contest for his piece, "How to Become Your Father." They have had to learn how to inhabit their body and therefore strive to enjoy it. They also enjoy caring for their bird's nest fern and watching professional wrestling with their loved ones.

Monica Sok is the author of *A Nail the Evening Hangs On* (Copper Canyon Press, 2020) and *Year Zero*, winner of a 2015 Poetry Society of

America Chapbook Fellowship. Her poems appear or are forthcoming in *American Poetry Review, The Best American Poetry 2021, Paris Review, POETRY, The Kenyon Review*, and others. She was born and raised in the Amish country of Lancaster, Pennsylvania and currently lives in New York City.

Joanna Solfrian's first book, *Visible Heavens*, was chosen by Naomi Shihab Nye for the 2009 Stan and Tom Wick Poetry Prize, a national first book award. Her second collection, *The Mud Room*, was published by MadHat Press, followed by the chapbook *The Second Perfect Number* by Finishing Line Press. In 2024 Beltway Editions will publish the collection *Temporary Beast*. Her poems have appeared in *The Harvard Review, Boulevard, Rattle, Margie, The Southern Review, Salamander, Pleiades, Image*, and elsewhere. She is a MacDowell Fellow and a five-time Pushcart nominee. Joanna lives and works in New York City. joannasolfrian.com

Donna Spruijt-Metz is the author of *General Release from the Beginning of the World* (2023, Free Verse Editions, Palette Press), an emeritus psychology professor, MacDowell fellow, rabbinical school drop-out, and former classical flutist. She was featured as one of '5 over 50 debut authors' in *Poets & Writers Magazine* (11/23). Her chapbooks include *Slippery Surfaces, And Haunt the World* (with Flower Conroy). and *Dear Ghost'* (winner, 2023 Harbor Review Editor's prize). Her poems appear or are forthcoming in The Academy of American Poets, *Poetry Northwest, Alaska Quarterly Review*, and elsewhere.

Heather Swan is a poet and nonfiction writer. Her poems have appeared in such journals as *The Hopper, One Art, Terrain, Poet Lore, Phoebe, The Raleigh Review*, and *Cold Mountain*. Her most recent collection *Dandelion* was just released from Terrapin Books. Her first book, *A Kinship with Ash* (Terrapin Books), published in 2020, was a finalist for both the ASLE Book Award and the Julie Suk Award. Her nonfiction book *Where Honeybees Thrive* (Penn State Press) won the Sigurd F. Olson Nature Writing Award.

Kelly Grace Thomas is a poet, writer, educator, and an ocean-obsessed Aries from Jersey. Her first full-length collection, *Boat Burned*, was released with YesYes Books in 2020. She is the winner of the Jane Underwood Poetry Prize and the Neil Postman Award for Metaphor. Kelly's poems have appeared in: *The Adroit Journal, Best New Poets, 32 Poems, Los Angeles Review, Sixth Finch,* and elsewhere. Kelly has received fellowships from Randolph College, the Martha's Vineyard Institute of Creative Writing and Kenyon Review Young Writers' Workshop. She lives in Benicia, California and is working on her first novel. kellygracethomas.com

Lynne Thompson served as the Los Angeles Poet Laureate, 2021-22, and received a Laureate Fellowship from the Academy of American Poets. She's the author of three collections of poetry, *Beg No Pardon, Start With a Small Guitar*, and *Fretwork*, as well as the forthcoming *Blue on A Blue Palette* (BOA Editions, 2024).

KC Trommer is the author of *We Call Them Beautiful* (Diode Editions, 2019) and *The Hasp Tongue* (dgp, 2014) and is founder of the online poetry project *QUEENSBOUND*. Since 2018, KC has collaborated with the Grammy Award-winning composer Herschel Garfein on a song cycle based on poems from her first collection, three of which were included in Garfein's 2023 classical music release *The Layers*. She is at work on her second collection of poems, *Paragones*, which looks at the work and lives of female-identifying artists from across the globe. She lives in Jackson Heights, Queens, with her son.

Michael Tyrell is the author of three books, most recently *The Arsonist's Letters* (Backlash, 2021). His work appears in *BOMB, Del Sol, The Night Heron Barks,* and *RE,* among other publications. He teaches writing at NYU.

Leah Umansky is the author of three collections of poetry, most recently, *Of Tyrant,* forthcoming with The Word Works in April 2024. She earned her MFA in Poetry at Sarah Lawrence College and has curated and hosted The COUPLET Reading Series in NYC since 2011. Her creative work can be found in such places as *The New York Times*, The Academy of American Poets *Poem-A Day*, *USA Today*, *POETRY*, and *American Poetry Review*. Her poem, "Reckoning" is an excerpt from her hybrid memoir, *Delicate Machine*, an exploration of womanhood, hope, and heart in the face of grief and a global pandemic. It is looking for a home. She can be found at leahumansky.com.

Barbara Ungar's sixth book, *After Naming the Animals*, is forthcoming from The Word Works. Prior books include *Save Our Ship*, which won the Snyder Prize from Ashland Poetry Press; *The Origin of the Milky Way*, which won the Gival Poetry Prize; *Immortal Medusa*, and *Charlotte Brontë, You Ruined My Life*. She has published recently in *Scientific American*, the *Comstock Review*, *Atticus Review*, *Cutthroat*, *Pedestal*, *Gargoyle*, and the journal formerly known as *Crazyhorse*. Her work has been translated into Spanish, Italian, Portuguese, and Bulgarian. The Standish Chair in English at The College of Saint Rose, she lives in Saratoga Springs, New York. barbaraungar.net

Lee Upton's most recent collection of poetry, *The Day Every Day Is*, was released from Saturnalia Books in 2023. Her novel *Tabitha, Get Up* is forthcoming in 2024.

Sara Wallace is the author of *The Rival* (selected for the Agha Shahid Ali Poetry Prize) and the chapbook *Edge* (selected for The Center for Book Arts Poetry Chapbook Competition). Her poetry has appeared in such publications as *Agni, Hanging Loose, Michigan Quarterly Review, Poetry Daily, Yale Review,* and others. A recent participant in the Festival Internacional de Poesia (Santiago, Chile), and a finalist for a Rona Jaffe Foundation Writer's Award, she is a recipient of grants from the New York Foundation for the Arts, the Sustainable Arts Foundation, as well as fellowships from the Virginia Center of the Creative Arts and the Millay Colony for the Arts. As a neurodivergent person with low-frequency hearing loss, she enjoys advocating for people with disabilities however she can. She currently teaches at New York University and lives with her family and cat, Taylor, in Queens.

Jessica L. Walsh is the author of *Book of Gods and Grudges* (Glass Lyre, 2022) as well as two previous collections and chapbooks. Her work has been featured in *RHINO, Guesthouse, Whale Road Review,* and on the Best American Poetry website, among others. Her poems have been nominated for the Pushcart Prize, Best of the Net, and Best New Poets. She grew up in small-town Michigan and hopes to move back, but for now she lives in suburban Chicago and teaches at a community college.

Patricia J. Wentzel (she/her/hers) lives at the confluence of two rivers and a satisfying life. She is a mental health and criminal justice advocate. She was a finalist for the Sublingual Prize for Poetry and her work is forthcoming in *Inverted Syntax, The Institutionalized Review,* and *The Tule Review.* She has been previously published in *Right Hand Pointing, The Monterey Poetry Review, Intima: a Journal of Narrative Medicine,* and others.

Zoë Ryder White's poems have appeared in *Tupelo Quarterly, Iterant,* and *Threepenny Review,* among others. Her chapbook, *Via Post,* was published in 2023 by Sixth Finch Press. *HYPERSPACE* was the editors' choice pick for the Verse Tomaž Šalamun Prize in 2020 and was published by Factory Hollow Press. She co-authored two chapbooks with Nicole Callihan: *A Study in Spring* and *Elsewhere.* A former elementary school teacher, she edits books for educators about the craft of teaching.

Ren Wilding earned an MA in Literature and Gender Studies from the University of Missouri. Their work has appeared in *Bellerive, The Outrider Review, Cactus Heart,* and *Trans Love: An Anthology of Transgender and Non-Binary Voices.* They were a finalist in the *Comstock*

Review's 2022 Chapbook Contest and winner of the St. Louis Poetry Center's 2023 James H. Nash Contest. Ren's poetry is rooted in the intersection of their identities as a queer, nonbinary, neurodivergent, and disabled human. They live in St. Louis with their wife and parrot.

Marianne Worthington is author of *The Girl Singer* (University Press of Kentucky, 2021), winner of the 2022 Weatherford Award for Poetry. Her work has appeared in *Oxford American, CALYX, Zone 3,* and *Swing,* among other places. She cofounded and is poetry editor of *Still: The Journal*, an online literary magazine publishing writers, artists, and musicians with ties to Appalachia since 2009. She grew up in Knoxville, Tennessee, and lives, writes, and teaches in southeastern Kentucky.

Justin Wymer is a poet and educator from West Virginia. His first poetry collection, *DEED*, won the Antivenom Poetry Award (Elixir, 2019). He has received awards and fellowships from the Radcliffe Institute, Harvard Office for the Arts, University of Denver, Academy of American Poets, and University of Iowa. He's an assistant professor of poetry at UT-Chattanooga. justinwymer.com

Editor Bios

Nicole Callihan (she/her) writes poems and stories. Her most recent book, *This Strange Garment*, navigates her 2020 breast cancer diagnosis and was published by Terrapin Books in March 2023. She is also the founder and curator of *Braving the Body*, an ongoing collaboration with Thomas Dooley's Poetry Well which invites poets to reflect on embodied experience and includes workshops, ekphrastic experiences, and the *Braving the Body* anthology. Her work has appeared in *Kenyon Review, Colorado Review, Conduit, The American Poetry Review*, and as a Poem-a-Day selection from the Academy of American Poets. A frequent collaborator with artists around the world, she has received support from the Rockefeller Foundation, Ludwig Vogelstein, and the Sustainable Arts Foundation. Winner of the 2023 Tenth Gate Prize and a 2023 Alma Award, Nicole Callihan has two forthcoming poetry collections: *chigger ridge* (The Word Works 2024) and *SLIP* (Saturnalia 2025). Find out more at nicolecallihan.com.

Pichchenda Bao (she/her) is a Cambodian American poet and writer, infant survivor of the Khmer Rouge genocide, daughter of refugees, and feminist stay-at-home mother. Her work has been published by *New Ohio Review*, *Cultural Daily*, and elsewhere. She has received support and fellowships from Queens Council on the Arts, Aspen Words, Bethany Arts Community, and Kundiman. She lives, writes, and raises her three children in New York City. More at pichchendabao.com

Jennifer Franklin (she/her) is the author of three full-length poetry collections including *If Some God Shakes Your House* (Four Way Books, 2023). Her work has been published widely in anthologies and journals including in *American Poetry Review*, *Macmillian's Bedford Introduction to Literature*, *The Nation*, *The Paris Review*, *Prairie Schooner*, Poetry Society's "Poetry in Motion" and The Academy of American Poets "poem-a-day" chosen by Diane Seuss. Franklin received a 2021 NYFA/City Artist Corps grant and a 2021 Café Royal Cultural Foundation Literature Award. She teaches craft workshops in Manhattanville's MFA program and manuscript revision at the Hudson Valley Writers Center, where she has served as Program Director for the past ten years. More at jenniferfranklinpoet.com.

About Small Harbor Publishing

Small Harbor Publishing is a 501c3 nonprofit organization. Our goal is to publish unique and diverse voices. We are a feminist press, and we are committed to diversity and inclusion. We strive to fiercely promote the work of our authors and to bring new voices to a devoted and expanding readership.

Small Harbor Publishing began in 2018 with the first issue of *Harbor Review*. The magazine is an online space where poetry and art converse. *Harbor Review* quickly grew and now publishes reviews and runs three micro chapbook competitions, the Washburn Prize, the Editor's Prize, and the Jewish American Woman's Prize.

In July 2020, Small Harbor Publishing was officially incorporated and began Harbor Editions. Harbor Editions accepts submissions through a chapbook open reading period, a hybrid chapbook open reading period, the Marginalia Series, and the Laureate Prize.

In 2023, Harbor Anthologies began with a mission to promote texts that explore social justice issues and highlight marginalized writers.

If you would like to support Small Harbor Publishing, please visit our "About" page at smallharborpublishing.com/about.

www.ingramcontent.com/pod-product-compliance
Lightning Source LLC
LaVergne TN
LVHW011919181224
799436LV00003B/552